CANON

THE HUMAN FACE

CANON

Global Responsibilities and
Local Decisions

PHILIP SANDOZ

PENGUIN BOOKS

Published by the Penguin Group
Penguin Books Ltd, 27 Wrights Lane, London w8 5tz, England
Penguin Books USA Inc., 375 Hudson Street, New York, New York 10014, USA
Penguin Books Australia Ltd, Ringwood, Victoria, Australia
Penguin Books Canada Ltd, 10 Alcorn Avenue, Toronto, Ontario, Canada m4v 3b2
Penguin Books (NZ) Ltd, 182–190 Wairau Road, Auckland 10, New Zealand

Penguin Books Ltd, Registered Offices: Harmondsworth, Middlesex, England

First published 1997
1 3 5 7 9 10 8 6 4 2
First edition

Copyright © IRI Inc., 1997

The moral right of the author has been asserted

Set in 11.5/14pt Monotype Bembo
Typeset by Rowland Phototypesetting Ltd, Bury St Edmunds, Suffolk
Printed in Great Britain by Clays Ltd, St Ives plc

A CIP catalogue record for this book is available from the British Library

ISBN 0-670-87408-6

This book is the second in the series *Japanese Business: The Human Face*, which will examine the most important companies in Japan today. These companies are all global leaders with multi-billion dollar turnovers and thousands of employees. Yet they face unprecedented challenges in the next few years. The pace of globalization, technical development, consumer expectation and growing international competition has never been faster. This series shows how the best and most successful are adapting and changing to remain in front. Each book describes the company's strategy, organization change, its impact on the workforce and, crucially, the importance of leadership in steering the company into the next millennium. These books contain crucial lessons for anyone interested in organizations, business and managing change.

Titles published in the series *Japanese Business: The Human Face*:
Mitsubishi Electric by Sol Sanders
Canon by Philip Sandoz

List of Illustrations

1. The office of Canon's predecessor, Seiki Kogaku Kenkyusho (Precision Optical Instruments Laboratory).

2. The Kwanon camera mark.

3. The Kwanon, Japan's first 35mm focal-plane-shutter camera.

4. Dr Takeshi Mitarai signs a contract with Jardine Matheson & Co. in 1951 for the exclusive distribution of all Canon products worldwide.

5. Dr Takeshi Mitarai and Takeo Maeda at a Sports Day in the 1950s.

6. The New York branch office, which opened in 1955.

7. The Canon booth at the Photokina Show in Cologne, Germany (1960).

8. The first Canonet camera is ceremoniously transported on its way to the domestic market.

9. Canonets being assembled at the Toride plant in 1961.

10. Dr Takeshi Mitarai shaking hands with Chairman Percy of the Bell & Howell Company.

11. The ceremony in Panama to mark the first foundations of Canon Latin America, Inc.

12. The Canola 130, the world's first ten-key electronic calculator.

13. Dr Takeshi Mitarai and Masaaki Kobayashi attending the 1968 opening ceremony of Canon Amerstdam N.V.

14. HRH Queen Elizabeth II on a tour of the Shimomaruko plant.

15. The New Year assembly in 1976: President Takeo Maeda tells the Canon workforce about the Premier Company Plan.

16. The world's first computerized single-lens reflex camera.

17. Canon cameras and lenses in use at a tennis tournament.

18. Tennis star John Newcombe in an advertisement for Canon USA.

19. Canon's first plain-paper copying machine.

20. Canon's first Bubble Jet Printer.

21. The world's first compact-sized laser beam printer.

22. Canon top management and an employee representative at the fiftieth anniversary celebrations in 1987.

23. President Ryuzaburo Kaku announces the *kyosei* philosophy in 1988.

24. Ryuzaburo Kaku attending the Caux Round Table in China.

25. Keizo Yamaji receives an honorary doctorate in science from Christopher Newport University, USA.

26. The Canon Ecology R&D Centre.

27. Japan's Emperor and Empress with Dr Hajime Mitarai at the ceremony of the Imperial Invention Prize in 1994.

28. Ryuzaburo Kaku is presented with the BS7750 certificate.

29. Fujio Mitarai and Hewlett-Packard's Lewis E. Platt unveiling

a rock with the word *kyosei* on it at Canon headquarters in Shimomaruko.

30. Richard Burke, chairman of the Canon Foundation, talking to professors from Holland and Japan.

31. Former US Ambassador Walter Mondale with Dr Fujio Mitarai at the new president's reception in February 1996.

32. A view of the Fuji-Susono Research Park.

CANON

PREFACE

When I was offered the chance to write a book on the human face of Japanese business, I jumped at it. I have lived in Japan for most of the past twenty-three years, and during this time I have worked with, and occasionally for, many Japanese companies, both large and small, famous and unknown.

The one thing almost all those companies had in common was the humanity of their people. I don't think I could have found quite so many encouraging and, occasionally, incorrigible people anywhere else in the world. Often referred to as inscrutable, the Japanese are far from it. A visitor only has to spend an evening being deafened by the roar of laughter in a cheap bar, or watch the weepy soaps on afternoon television, to encounter a whole range of heartfelt emotions. The Japanese are, in fact, very scrutable.

Corporate Japan, on the other hand, can be a little hard to get to know. Experience will show the Japan watcher that when you get a Japanese alone, you can have an interesting and wide-ranging discussion, but put a group of them together, and nobody is going to say anything he isn't certain will meet with the others' total approval. Getting to know an organization, therefore, can be difficult.

The vast majority of Japanese companies don't want to be investigated, particularly by a *gaijin* (foreigner – literally, outsider). This is not necessarily because they have any skeletons in the cupboard, but mainly because they are a little bit ashamed that the cupboard may not be perfectly clean. On the whole, I don't think Japanese business people are any more or less honest and decent than those in any other country, but they are usually much more careful about what they say.

There are a few exceptions, and these tend to be the newer, mainly post-war corporations, such as Sony and Honda. Both these companies were founded and have been led by extrovert visionaries, who have done brilliant work in publicizing their companies and themselves. And both companies have one other thing in common: they are possibly even better known and more respected outside Japan than within. They are, perhaps, a little too extrovert for the Japanese to take them truly to their hearts.

In some ways similar to Sony and Honda, but in many ways almost diametrically opposed, is Canon Inc. It is a post-war company that has been led by a procession of visionaries, but unlike the other two, Canon has managed to retain its very strong Japanese identity while at the same time taking on the trappings of whatever society it has joined on a global scale.

While this book was being researched and written, the chairman of Canon was Ryuzaburo Kaku, a true philosopher and long-term planner. Though he is no longer in a position of exerting executive power within the company, he remains a member of the board and will continue to have an effect on Canon through the continuance of his *kyosei* (living and working together for the common good) philosophy. His influence on the company, particularly since the dark days of 1975 when it was unable, for the first time in its history, to pay a shareholders' dividend, is beyond measure. I wish him many more years of health and hope his dreams of *kyosei* are ultimately realized.

Also of critical value to Canon is the current president, Fujio Mitarai. The nephew of the founder, Takeshi Mitarai, Fujio has the wit and ability to move Canon forward in a world of globalization. Having lived outside Japan for twenty-three years, he knows what to expect, and relishes the challenges. His openness, both with his colleagues and this writer, is exceptional. Again, I thank him.

Canon claims to be more open than most Japanese companies, and says it welcomes constructive criticism and debate, from inside the company as well as from outside commentators. I must admit, I was impressed with the open attitudes of almost everyone I met at Canon, from the youngest secretaries to the chairman. What was particularly interesting for me was that they never appeared to toe a party line. When asked a question, they generally responded from their hearts – not from the company rule-book. For this I thank them.

Finally, I have often been disappointed when I read business books about Japan or Japanese corporations. They usually leave me hungering for more, because they don't let the protagonists speak. In this book, with the exception of the final chapter, I have tried to keep my voice to a minimum, and let the people who really know about Canon tell you what they think is interesting.

I hope you find it interesting too.

Philip Sandoz
Tokyo, March 1997

CHAPTER ONE

Finding the headquarters of Canon Inc. in the tiny Tokyo suburb of Shimomaruko is easy. All the potential visitor has to do is follow the crowds on the ten-minute walk from the tiny railway station along a traditionally noisy Japanese shopping street to the headquarters compound. You can't make a mistake, because there really is nowhere else to go and nothing else worth seeing in Shimomaruko. Just about everyone you see will be wearing Canon's corporate lapel badge, so even following the wrong person is practically impossible.

Arriving at the entrance to the headquarters of one of the world's leading companies may come as a slight shock to even the most experienced of global businessmen. At the gate – a gate like that at the entrance to any factory throughout the world – the visitor's first thought is that there must have been a mistake, or perhaps the instructions hadn't been completely understood.

Nothing at the entrance suggests a headquarters establishment, and the view from the gate is of squat, warehouse-like buildings with obvious industrial origins. And the guards don't help. The non-Japanese speaker is left to stare in incredulity until one of the smartly uniformed girls in what can only be described as a military-style guardhouse asks, in passable English, if she can help.

Once you have managed to explain who you want to see, and filled out the untidily copied questionnaire in English, you have a few seconds to ponder on why a leading printer manufacturer couldn't prepare a better form, before being given a badge and told to report to reception in the headquarters building.

Canon's headquarters building is a fourteen-storey block rising incongruously from what obviously used to be a manufacturing plant. Between the guardhouse and the HQ the visitor will pass a couple of warehouses, the company's convenience store and the in-plant bicycle store, before passing the bronze bust of founder Dr Takeshi Mitarai to the left of the HQ's supermarket-like revolving doors. If you visit early on a Monday morning, you can even see Dr Mitarai getting a wash and brush-up from corporate cleaning staff.

On entering the headquarters, you will report to the second reception and be asked to wait until you are collected by a member of Canon's staff. If from reception you are taken to the lift on the right, you are obviously headed for the realms of the gods, but if you are guided to the lift on the left, it is clearly for more mundane business. Those lucky enough to travel on the right-hand elevator will be whisked speedily and silently to the fourteenth floor where silence, tranquillity and beautiful displays of ceramics and other Japanese art set the scene for a meeting with the powerful. Strangely though, considering this is the headquarters of a world-leading camera manufacturer, there are very few photographs on show.

Through the windows of the fourteenth floor, however, can be seen something even better than a photograph. The gorgeous and breathtaking panorama includes the snow-capped beauty of Mount Fuji on one side and the Manhattan-like skyline of Shinjuku, one of metropolitan Tokyo's leading business and entertainment districts, on the other. Looking down from the eyrie of Canon's top executives, the observer will see a hive of activity, with hundreds of headquarters workers scurrying to and fro on the business of one of Japan's, and the world's, leading high-technology companies. But the majestic silence of the fourteenth floor makes it almost impossible to believe that the people inhabiting this sanctuary of tranquillity actually successfully soil their hands with mere commerce.

Despite this image of cultured removal from the business world, however, the directors of Canon today are totally in touch with that world. A little over twenty years ago, the visitor's initial judgment may have been closer to what was then the truth. In the spring of 1975, almost forty years after the founding of Canon, the directors had brought the company almost to its knees. For the first time in its history, Canon found itself unable to pay a dividend to shareholders. In reality, the company could have paid, but having issued a series of bonds on the London market, Canon had to abide by the rules governing international financial transactions which disallow the payment of dividends from accumulated profits. For the first time ever, therefore, Canon was in the embarrassing position of appearing unable to meet its commitments. And in a show of unusual aggression the Japanese press blew the molehill up into a mountain, making Canon's future look distinctly doubtful. Although, according to Tomomasa Matsui, a retired managing director, 'Since the war the business had been cyclical, and, in fact, the general trend was up, and the accounts department was telling everyone the so-called crisis was no big deal', morale plummeted, and the board finally decided that something had at least to be seen to be done about the situation.

Surrounded by rumours and gossip at head office, the directors decided to meet *in camera* at the Prince Hotel, a Western-style hotel in Shinagawa, a move which in fact added fuel to the workers' sense of panic. Says Matsui, 'The fact that we met privately in a hotel backfired on us, as it was almost the same as broadcasting that there was a crisis big enough to demand secrecy.'

In reality, the choice of a Western hotel was logical. Japanese-style inns have rooms for meetings, but domestic hospitality demands that there is a constant supply of food and drinks, and the room is never free from serving women. In a Western-style hotel room, on the other hand, guests are left alone unless something is ordered.

There wasn't much for the participants to enjoy at the meeting, and they certainly wouldn't have felt like baring their souls in front of serving women. On the whole it was a very sombre occasion. Ryuzaburo Kaku, later chairman, then one of the lowest-ranked directors attending, even goes so far as to say he found the first session boring. Since this meeting was critical to both Kaku's career and Canon's future, it is best to hear the story in his own words.

'In 1975, when we realized we couldn't pay a stockholders' dividend, all the senior management was called to a secret emergency meeting at the Prince Hotel in Shinagawa. The agenda was very simple; we had to decide how to overcome the crisis and get Canon back on its feet. The trouble had come about through a combination of factors, but the main problems had been the failure of our electronic calculator business, and – there's no other way to put it – general mismanagement and lack of foresight throughout the company.

'The mismanagement was chronic, with nobody seeming to know what the company should do and individual directors countermanding the orders of others. It was as if Canon ordered its workers to march to Mount Fuji, out there to the west. If told to do so, they would all face in that direction and set off. Admittedly, some would move faster than others, but they would all be treading the same path. But then, what if someone rescinded that order and told them that they had to go to Mount Tsukuba, to the east of Tokyo, instead? The workers, being loyal, would about-face and get moving again. But, after a number of such illogical changes, the workers, not being stupid, would realize it would be easier just to wait in Tokyo, and make no further efforts whatsoever until the parade passed again. They would lose faith as they saw their efforts coming to nothing. That was really how Canon was being managed before the crisis meeting. It was no wonder the company was in trouble and fast approaching a crisis.

'I was the most junior managing director to be in on the meeting and, though I wasn't over-awed, I decided it would be better to bide my time and just keep my mouth shut for a while. We knew the meeting was going to go on for a long time, and in fact it eventually lasted for two complete days. During the first morning I kept quiet and just listened to my seniors. I didn't say a single word as the directors, in order of seniority, delivered their speeches one after the other. It was a complete waste of time. They were just making presentations and there was no real discussion of the problems.

'However, it was not my place to complain and I thought the rest of the meeting would pass in the same way. Then the president, apparently having noticed my silence, said, "You haven't said a word! What did you come for? The free lunch?" I apologized and explained that I had been listening to the ideas of my superiors, but, I told him, if he wanted to genuinely hear my opinions, I wouldn't have the slightest hesitation to give them in very plain words.

'Once I started, I couldn't stop. I outlined my concept of the Premier Company Plan and explained to all present what would be necessary to revitalize Canon. I told them that since joining the company over twenty years before, in 1954, I had made many, many proposals concerning the way things could be improved, but not a single one of them had been acted on. Perhaps I was a little blunt, but I told them that if they had acted on my proposals the company wouldn't be in the mess we were then discussing, and we would already be running an excellent company. This took me all of what remained of the first day.

'On the second day of the meeting I explained each aspect of my proposals in turn, and went into details on how they should be implemented. As I saw it, the biggest problem with Canon at the time was old-fashioned managers who hadn't realized the world had changed, and who couldn't think of anything except cameras. They believed the company should drop everything else and concentrate on our core strength, cameras and lenses. There was, however, a second group that wanted change, and the battle between these two groups had been going on at all levels of the board for over ten years.

'I, of course, was a supporter of the group that wanted diversification and change, so I based all my presentation on the subject of growth through new businesses. It is true that Canon had started to diversify with the introduction of electronic calculators and through the development of the Synchroreader recording device and other products, but both attempts had been doomed to failure through lack of top management enthusiasm. Inactivity can kill a product just as surely as rushing it out too early.

'I told them that we would have to use the hotel meeting as the starting point of uniting top management. And that was what it was; only the starting point. The story of this meeting is sometimes told as if the board was enlightened like St Paul on the road to Damascus, but this is ridiculous. Attitudes that have been fought over for ten years don't change overnight, but suffice it to say, the inability to pay a dividend, followed by this extra-special meeting, was enough of a shock to make even the most die-hard traditionalists think again. Once I sat down, there was a lively discussion. Not the discussion of one group against the other, but that of people really trying to make an accommodation.'

In this move, the relatively inexperienced board member, Kaku, had done something that can best be described as very un-Japanese. He had confronted not only the problems facing the company, but also the people he felt had caused the crisis. And not only had it worked, but it set both Canon and Kaku moving along new paths – Canon to profitability, Kaku to eventual chairmanship.

The corporate culture of open discussion that the directors adopted during that two-day marathon meeting is one of the most prized attributes of Canon today. For example, in most Japanese companies managers are always referred to by their position and name, for example, Manager Suzuki or Section Head Okazaki, but at Canon the management are generally simply addressed as Mr or Ms, thus Suzuki-san and Okazaki-san. This may seem an unimportant distinction, but in a land of rigid social structures it is considerably easier to talk openly to a Mr or a Ms than to a designated superior.

After Kaku's explanation, president Maeda and the other board members decided to take the road of diversification which allowed Canon to grow rapidly and healthily for the next twenty years. With a typical lack of modesty, indeed with unconcealed pride, Kaku explains. 'It is easy to see what my plan has brought. In 1975 Canon was ranked 867 in the *Fortune* league of top industrial companies, with sales of $401 million. Xerox, ranked 80, had sales of $40.94 billion, and Kodak, at 60, totalled $49.58 billion. Canon had less than a tenth of the sales of those two companies. In *Fortune*'s 1995 list Canon was ranked 60, with sales of $230.12 billion; Xerox, at 71, had sales of $189 billion; and Kodak, at 106, $152 billion. Xerox, therefore, had sales 4.6 times greater in 1994 than in 1974, and Kodak had increased sales by 3.1 times. Canon, on the other hand, had overtaken both companies and had sales fifty-seven times bigger than twenty years before. Now, that is what I call successful growth.'

It is indeed very successful, but one of the results of these decades of phenomenal growth and diversification is that it is extremely difficult to compare Canon with competitive corporations. In fact the company has such a wide spread of products that it cannot be said to have any one competitor. A study of the domestic market shares of some of Canon's major product groups, however, sheds some interesting light on the company's strengths. In the manufacture of stepper machines for the semiconductor industry, the market is dominated by Nikon, with approximately 64 per cent of the market (1995 figures). Canon comes in second with around 34.5 per cent, leaving all other manufacturers the crumbs of a mere 1.5 per cent of the market.

In facsimile manufacture Canon again ranks second, but this time the race is much closer. First is Ricoh (17 per cent in 1995), then Canon (14.4 per cent), followed by Matsushita Graphic Communication (14 per cent), NEC (12 per cent) and TEC (8.5 per cent). In ink jet printers, Canon, with 33.9 per cent of the market, once again is just off the top position which is held by Seiko Epson with 36.1 per cent. The next nearest competitor here is NEC, with a significant but comparatively lowly 14.8 per cent.

When it comes to plain paper copiers, believe it or not, Canon again comes in in second position with 28 per cent of the 1995 market, beaten by Ricoh (31.3 per cent) and followed by Fuji Xerox (25 per cent) and Sharp (8 per cent).

Only in cameras, apparently, does Canon eschew the number two position. In the manufacture of single-lens reflex cameras, Canon is the leader, with 36.4 per cent of the market in 1995, followed by Minolta (23.7 per cent), Nikon (16.5 per cent), Asahi Optical (9.5 per cent) and Kyocera (4.8 per cent). In the area of compact cameras, however, Canon drops to third position with 12 per cent of the market in 1995, topped by Fuji Photo Film (23 per cent) and Olympus Optical (15.7 per cent), and trailed by Konica (11.7 per cent), Asahi Optical (10.4 per cent) and Minolta (9.1 per cent). Incidentally, in the previous year Canon was in second place in this market, too, but lost out after a significant spurt of growth by Olympus Optical. However, the current extremely successful sales of the company's new IXY compact camera will more than likely restore it to second place when the 1996 figures are revealed.

So, of the six major product areas mentioned, Canon ranks second in four, beaten by Ricoh in two cases, and by Seiko Epson and Nikon in the other two. In the two most significant areas of camera manufacture, Canon leads in the SLR field and is bested by two competitors, Fuji Photo Film and Olympus Optical, in compact camera sales.

What we have here, therefore, is a truly diverse manufacturer that is competitive across a broad spectrum of products, and which cannot be easily compared with any single competitor company. In fact, this is what Chairman Kaku claims to be a premier company.

The Premier Company Plan (in Japanese, *yuryo kigyo*), claims Kaku, is often mistranslated as 'Blue-chip Company Plan', a description he strongly disagrees with. 'A blue-chip company is one with owned capital, excellent finances; a company which returns considerable profits to its shareholders or to capital. Of course, from a financial point of view, this meaning is included in the term *yuryo kigyo*, but from the point of view of purpose the terms are quite different. Canon's *yuryo kigyo* plan is fundamentally a philosophy aimed at serving the human race and the world through the company's actions. This objective is often misunderstood.'

According to Kaku, the *yuryo kigyo* plan was adopted because Canon wanted a policy that would never need to be changed. Initially, because of the previous year's shortfall, the aims of the plan were mainly financial. The first objective, starting in 1976, was for Canon to increase net income by 10 per cent against sales a year and become a totally loan-free company. How these goals were achieved is an example of the originality that is now a signal strength of the company in research and development and other departments. Kaku explains, 'Japan already had its own blue-chip companies, but to try to improve Canon through blind imitation of Toyota or Matsushita, for example, wasn't even an alternative. Anyone who ever tries to imitate a genius learns this lesson very quickly.'

The case studies of other corporations gave Canon hints of strategies, but the new so-called 'Canon-style' production system was unique, including total quality control in everything from products to finances to personnel. In production, for example, Canon devised a system to eliminate nine wastes: in preparatory work, defective goods, facilities, expenses, management, design, human resources, mobility, and initiation of production. And it worked. Production costs were reduced by $16 million in 1976 and by $28.2 million in 1977.

Other areas targeted specifically in 1976 were research and development operations, employee education and marketing strategies. Says Kaku: 'Although R & D was operating relatively smoothly at the time, we set to doubling its efficiency: in other words, cutting R & D time in half. In the educational field, we laid the programme for our International Operations Headquarters, which nowadays trains managerial staff for positions abroad and provides educational seminars for overseas managers brought specially to Japan.

'Within its first year the *yuryo kigyo* plan had permeated virtually all operations of Canon, and we saw no reason why the Canon group should not now take the steps that would make it one of Japan's true blue-chip companies. We drew up plans under which certain subsidiaries would become departments of the parent company while others would be made totally independent. Both Canon Electronics Inc. and Canon Sales Co., Inc. were listed separately on the Tokyo Stock Exchange.'

In the next stage of achieving the *yuryo kigyo* plan at Canon, 1978 saw the introduction of a matrix system of management. For many years the company had been suffering from a bottleneck situation. This was the direct result of the rapid growth from small, almost single-product company to large general manufacturer. In many cases only a single person – often only the president – could make an important decision which might affect almost all of the company. This style of management is probably satisfactory in a single-product manufacturer, but is not suitable for a diversified maker, as the person in charge has less and less time to give to each product as the number of items produced regularly increases.

A typical example of this occurred when Canon introduced its electronic calculators. At that time the company was also producing cameras, optical and micrographic equipment, business equipment, and medical machines, so it was natural that the then president could not devote much time to the new range of products. The result was catastrophic. Canon launched the wrong products at the wrong time and at the wrong price. Competitors quickly caught up with and passed Canon's originally superior technology, and the company was left with warehouses full of unwanted products and a serious cash-flow problem.

Nowadays, the main management feature of Canon is its three-dimensional matrix system. A divisional organization by product group permits the flow of work to progress among functional units of each group or profit centre. A divisional manager is responsible for the total programmes of work involving the products of his or her division. Linking these divisions are functional committees which seek to improve and coordinate development, production and marketing. The third dimension of the matrix coordinates operations on a geographic basis, mainly through regional headquarters such as those in Shimomaruko (for Japan and Asia), New York (for the Americas) and Amsterdam (for Europe). Even within this system, however, some areas of particular strength are given even more autonomy, including, for example, Canon UK and Canon East Europe. The matrix structure serves as an effective mechanism for managing the complexities of rapid diversification, enhanced vertical integration and internationalization. It allows the complete organization the flexibility and versatility required for rapid response to changes in technology and the environment. A strong headquarters organization coordinates the activities of the autonomous divisions and regional organizations with the help of functional committees, and provides cohesion and direction to overall operations.

Prior to the introduction of the matrix system, Canon was a little like a team of horses all pulling in different directions and with a driver unable to keep them under control. By the end of 1978, however, Canon felt it had learnt to control the team through the introduction of a reasonably efficient worldwide management system. The company then decided that the next two years should be spent focusing on achieving the *yuryo kigyo* plan on the home front. But, explains Kaku, 'We decided, instead of simply operating to benefit employees, Canon would make a commitment to work for the betterment of the entire human race.' This may sound all well and good, but what does it really mean? After all, it is not really very unusual to hear such sentiments from companies, governments and bureaucracies, each invariably claiming to be working for the betterment of society: but, of course, when the chips are down, nothing really changes.

There is no doubt that Canon's claims leave the company wide open to both Western and Japanese cynicism. However, it is important to remember that Chairman Kaku, a survivor of the Nagasaki atomic bombing, may have a slightly different outlook on life, and genuinely not really care for the promotion of images and the use of empty words. And it is not only Kaku who thinks this way. Since the days of the introduction of the Premier Company Plan, some things have not changed. Current Canon President Fujio Mitarai is obviously the strongest supporter of corporate morals, and in complete agreement with his corporate figurehead.

Humanistic philosophy is not generally the businessman's strong point, but Ryuzaburo Kaku is clearly an exception. 'Corporate social responsibility doesn't end at making monetary donations to a local welfare institution. The greatest way for a company to serve society is to employ as many citizens as possible. And to do that we have to make profits, because it is only through profits that reinvestment, expansion and more employment are possible. This is Canon's mission – to expand employment throughout the world, whether it be in France, Germany, the US, Australia or China.

'In the past Japanese companies have tended to pump all profits made by subsidiaries on foreign soil back into the Tokyo home office. This approach to expansion ignores a corporation's responsibility to the livelihood of the host country and, more importantly, to the local employees. To correct this trend, Canon has changed its overall stance to enable overseas subsidiaries to share profits and achieve a higher degree of independence.'

As will be seen in the following chapters, Canon has an almost missionary-like zeal for the propagation of ethical business, but it is important to understand that Canon's leaders are first and foremost genuine businessmen, not evangelists who happen to be in business. The company may have strong beliefs, but they are business beliefs. Canon understands that it exists only to do business and, therefore, must temper its idealistic dreams with a touch of reality. And this is exactly what the company has been doing. The results have been positive. As Kaku explains: 'Over the years the Premier Company Plan has evolved, but there have always been three pillars. First, there must be a clearly defined management philosophy, and Canon has adopted *kyosei*, a business philosophy that can best be translated as living and working together for the common good. Second, at least 10 per cent of non-consolidated sales mut be annually invested in research and development. The positive results of this spending can best be shown by Canon's position in the league of US patents granted. In 1986 we were fifth, in '87 we rose to first, from then until '90 we stayed in third position, and in '91 we slipped to fifth. But in '92, as a result of a severe talking-to, our engineers got us back to number one, where we belong. The third pillar of our corporate philosophy has been to be ready for any strengthening of the yen. Because of this, we have moved much of our operations abroad, and are looking to increase our global presence even further in the coming years.'

Furthermore, this increase in global presence is intended to be attained through a system of global and strategic partnerships, of which Canon has had much experience. Not belonging to a *zaibatsu*, a broad business group often including manufacturers, service companies and at least one bank, Canon has had to go it alone. In the past, partnerships with companies such as Jardine Matheson in sales and Hewlett-Packard in production have proved very successful outside Japan. Within the Japanese market Canon has also had several successes, including being the first sole-distributor to introduce Apple Computers to the domestic scene. Even today, Canon still has a considerable stake in the success of this company. Instead of relying on sales from and by *zaibatsu* group companies, Canon has been forced to find many international partners, and, its management says, prefers the sight of the clear blue water between Canon and most of the other incestuous leading Japanese companies.

These high ideals sound wonderful, but are they just propaganda? Before a company can talk of global equality, it has to stand strong on its own base. In Japan, has Canon proved to be an employer worthy of international respect, or are we just witness again to a whitewash job of international relations? The origins and personalities of Canon will tell.

CHAPTER TWO

A Friday or Saturday evening walk through Tokyo's Roppongi entertainment district with its kaleidoscopic neon, cacophonic roar of bar owners, restaurateurs and pimps, and the sheer struggle of trying to make headway in a sea of drunken salaried workers, good-time boys and girls, American and European stockbrokers out to exercise their expense accounts, and GIs out for other exercises, makes it hard to believe that this was once the home of Japan's bureaucracy, and the original site of a camera manufacturer which named its products, with only the slightest of spelling changes, after Kannon, the Buddhist Goddess of Mercy.

November 1933, in a Japan very different from today, saw the newly founded Seiki Kogaku Kenkyusho (Precision Instruments Laboratory), SKK, set up shop in Roppongi. Started by a former Yamaichi Securities employee, Saburo Uchida, and his partner and brother-in-law, Goro Yoshida, there seemed to be little rationale behind the company. Uchida, apparently knowing little about cameras, had not even been keen to become involved in the beginning. But his belief that the only way resource-starved Japan could compete on international markets was through investment in high technology and intelligent planning soon overcame his initial hesitance.

By June 1934 *Asahi Camera*, a leading photographic magazine, was carrying a far from modest advertisement for the fledgling company. In a pointed parallel to Japan's rapidly burgeoning military expansionism and hegemony, the advertisement read:

The Best in the World: Igo for Submarines,
Model 92 for Aircraft and KWANON for Cameras.

Despite this apparent pride, however, SKK was not making a camera even approaching the quality of the German Leica or Contax models. Even if it had, it is highly unlikely that many would have been sold. In 1934 the top-of-the-range Japanese Pearl spring camera was retailing for around ¥49 ($14.5 as of 1934), whereas the top Leica, Model II, sold for ¥420 ($123.9). With a college-graduated bank employee earning around ¥70 ($20.6) monthly there simply wasn't a large potential market for the quality product. Despite the lack of both products and markets, however, Uchida was not put off and over the next couple of years hired several excellent engineers and designers to work on his Kwanon range of cameras and lenses.

Uchida's genius was not so much, perhaps, in his engineering or marketing skills as in his ability to enthuse and bring on board the varied talents that would eventually make Canon the leading and most innovative of Japanese technology companies. In 1934, for example, he recruited Takeo Maeda, a former subordinate at Yamaichi Securities. Maeda was a talented administrator and soon had the fledgling company organized. He was eventually to succeed Mitarai as its president.

But Uchida's greatest success may well have been the fact that he brought on board his friend Takeshi Mitarai, the first member of a family that, along with many talented researchers, would take Canon into the forefront of Japanese industry and is still represented by current company president, Fujio Mitarai. Takeshi Mitarai was born on Kyushu, Japan's southern main island, but in a display of wanderlust that was later to become a hallmark of Canon, he studied medicine on the northern main island, at Hokkaido Imperial University, before moving to Tokyo and working in obstetrics and gynaecology at the Japan Red Cross

Hospital, near the newly opened offices of SKK. It is not exactly clear where the two men originally met, but they had evidently become close friends by the late 1930s when Uchida set about convincing his friend to back-pedal slightly on his medical ambitions, and join him in a partnership at SKK.

Mitarai's career in medicine (he became an MD in 1937) had stimulated his interest in medical imaging, particularly X-rays. While out drinking one evening, he became involved in a discussion centring on the worldwide renown of German precision industries, particularly in imaging, and Japan's relative lack of success in the same fields. Mitarai became so fired up with the idea of Japan equalling and then beating the Germans in this area that he was eventually persuaded to join his friend Uchida at SKK. Initially he was only a financial investor in the company, and it was several years before he was persuaded to take a more active role in management. In many ways he saw himself first and foremost as a man of medicine rather than as a businessman. In those early years, and to a lesser degree for the rest of his life, he insisted that SKK was only one part of his life and continued his medical career, eventually setting up the Mitarai Obstetrics and Gynaecology Hospital in Tokyo in 1940.

Even before Mitarai got on board, however, SKK had gone through various incarnations and changes of direction. The first major disagreement was between the two original founders, Yoshida and Uchida. Yoshida, as the originator, initially had the upper hand, and it was he who decided to name the cameras after the Buddhist Goddess of Mercy, Kannon, and the range of lenses after a Buddhist wise man, Mahakasyapa. Yoshida even designed the company's first logo in line with his Buddhist faith, and for several years a supposedly high technology-oriented company was represented by the image of the thousand-handed Kannon amidst flame-shaped lettering.

Uchida, though initially brought into the company by Yoshida, soon took a distinctly antagonistic approach to many of the latter's ideas, particularly those bearing on the founder's religious beliefs. Little by little Uchida started to modernize the company. SKK began to operate more like a genuine business concern as Uchida's realism took over from Yoshida's idealism.

The watershed in relations between the two was reached in 1934, when Uchida expressed a strong dislike of Yoshida's choice of the name Kwanon. The reason behind it was probably that religious overtones should not be present in the industry, particularly when a company was intending to produce high-technology products at the top end of the market. An argument followed during which Yoshida grew frustrated about the direction in which the company was moving and claimed that his idealism had been perverted. The outcome was predictable – practical business won out over idealism and Yoshida resigned from the company less than a year after he had founded it.

Uchida, once again in sole charge, was left to decide on how to erase the religious aspect of the company and what to do with the product names that would be relatively unknown in the West and appear obviously Buddhist to anyone in the East. In a stroke of marketing genius he struck on the idea of changing the Goddess Kannon to Canon, a word defined as 'a standard to judge by; a criterion' (*Webster's New World Dictionary*), which he felt was much more in line with a top-of-the-range manufacturer.

By October 1935 the name Canon was being pushed to the public. *Asahi Camera* carried an item stating:

> Hansa Canon camera . . . Canon is a Japanese-made imitation of Leica. It is similar to Leica in most parts although the influence of Contax on its mechanism cannot be overlooked . . . ¥275 [$81.1] with a snapshot case included.

In less than a year from its founding, SKK had produced a camera that was not only over five-and-a-half times the price of the market-leading Japanese Pearl camera, but, at least to the Japanese professional media, was technologically on the same level as Leica and Contax. What was even better for the fledgling company was the fact that with the emergence of several domestic film manufacturers and other camera makers, the Japanese market was going through a period of extremely healthy growth and rapid innovation, with SKK at its head. The Hansa Canon was only half the price of a comparable Leica but was undoubtedly a high-quality product. Significantly, the design of the Hansa Canon is regarded as the origin of the single-lens reflex (SLR) cameras still available on the market today.

During this period of the late thirties, as Japan caught up with and then overtook many countries in the area of high technology, it was also lurching towards a political system of military-led fascism that eventually plunged the whole of Asia into war and led inevitably, via the death camps of the Japanese conquest of Burma and elsewhere, to the carnage and destruction of Hiroshima and Nagasaki. But at SKK the mood was upbeat and political reality was only brought home in July 1937.

In that month Uchida had intended to relaunch the company, renamed in 1936 Nippon Seiki Kogaku Kenkyusho (Japan Precision Optical Laboratory) in a burst of patriotism. His plans were delayed for a month, however, as were most domestic business activities, after a clash between Japanese and Chinese troops just north of Peking. In what became known as the Marco Polo Bridge Incident, the Japanese troops, by this time completely beyond the control of the Tokyo government, deliberately brought about a clash with the Chinese army that, unlike several earlier incidents, turned out to be the last straw, causing a rapid escalation into full-scale war.

Despite the onset of hostilities, normal business in Japan resumed in just over a month, and on 10 August 1937 a new joint-stock company, with yet another new name, was formed with an initial capital of ¥1 million ($28,813). This date is now recognized as the official founding of Canon. With the formation of the new company, Seiki Kogaku Kogyo (Precision Optical Industry) Co. Ltd, Uchida had finally removed the idealism of Yoshida's 'laboratory' and replaced it with the much more businesslike 'Co. Ltd'. It certainly sounded more efficient, but in truth business could at best be described as erratic. In fact camera production during the run-up to the Second World War, when the nation had priorities considerably removed from leisure activities, ranged from as little as one a week to as high as ten a month. Hardly a burgeoning production rate.

And things didn't improve. On 8 December 1941 Japan attacked Pearl Harbor and brought the United States into the war. Ironically, the fall of Singapore to the Japanese on 15 February 1942 was to have a direct effect on the development of Canon. Immediately after the takeover, Uchida was ordered by the Japanese government to go to Singapore where he was to act as a consultant on civil administration to the Occupation Forces. Not knowing how long this appointment was to last, Uchida asked Mitarai to take over as head of SKK. The doctor, now with his own newly opened hospital in Tokyo, was initially against the idea, but eventually bowed to the inevitable and was appointed representative director in September 1942.

When finally in charge, Mitarai, although continuing to run his hospital, took his responsibilities very seriously. Under his management the company became more efficient and was running as well as could be expected in wartime conditions when Uchida returned from Singapore in spring 1943 and immediately demanded the restitution of his powers – he wanted to take sole charge of the company again. Many, however, were not convinced that Uchida would, after his time away, be able to perform well as chief executive. During his absence various things had changed, including the not insignificant fact that the import of foreign cameras, previously at a high level, had been banned from the Japanese market, thus leaving the field open – in theory at least – for companies like Canon. Mitarai obviously wanted to grasp the opportunity and expand, while Uchida was for a more tentative approach. Although history ultimately proved Mitarai correct, he was not really an in-fighter, and after several disagreements with Uchida he did indeed step down as representative director on 31 July 1943.

But the arguments continued, particularly over the expansion of the company through the purchase of Yamato Optical Manufacturing Co. Ltd, which Uchida opposed and Mitarai supported. The situation again came to a head, and on 13 September, a mere forty-five days after re-assuming power, Uchida realized that, though he may have been the victor in the seniority battle, he could not win the modernization war, and Mitarai was once more named representative director. Although Uchida remained a director, also taking the position of non-representative chairman, the relationship was never to recover, and Uchida finally severed his ties with the company on 15 October 1947, leaving the company in the capable hands of the Mitarai line.

Under the leadership of Dr Mitarai, SKK began to take on the form and philosophies recognizable in the Canon of today. Up until his death in October 1984, while still chairman of Canon, Takeshi Mitarai was responsible for instilling a code of ethics in his employees that is perhaps unrivalled in any leading Japanese company. In an interview in 1979 he explained his philosophy: 'Naturally, we have a responsibility to our stockholders to make a profit. But I feel that profitability alone is simply not enough. We also have an obligation to lend our strength to society's betterment.'

The obligation Dr Mitarai felt towards society is probably derived from his training as a physician. It is true that he was originally connected with a company that was simply attempting to take the technological lead in photography then held by the Germans. But within a few years of his joining forces with Uchida, the medical applications of imaging were assuming an increasingly important role in the company's development. In 1940, for example, the company produced and marketed an indirect X-ray camera for mass chest examinations in an attempt to counter the then-growing problem of tuberculosis. It was the first domestically produced indirect X-ray camera and, much to Dr Mitarai's delight, played a dramatic part in reducing tuberculosis in Japan. This was one of Canon's first moves to make a direct contribution to the bettering of society in general.

Looking at Canon nowadays, it is relatively easy to see how the foresightedness of Dr Mitarai has shaped the company. As of the end of the 1996 financial year, Canon's global work-force of 75,628 gave the company a consolidated net income of $812 million from total sales of $22.054 billion. Of these totals, business machines (copiers, computer peripherals, information systems) accounted for 83.6 per cent; optical and other products (including medical equipment) provided 8 per cent; and cameras gave 8.4 per cent. Expenditure on R&D was in excess of 12 per cent of total non-consolidated sales, resulting in Canon taking second place in the league tables of companies winning US patents.

In fact, Canon (1,541 patents granted) was only beaten by IBM (1,867), with the nearest Japanese competitor being NEC Corp. (1,043). Significantly, the top ten of the US patent league included only two American companies (IBM and Motorola: total 2,931 patents granted), with Japanese companies (Canon, NEC, Hitachi, Mitsubishi Electric, Toshiba, Fujitsu, Sony and Matsushita) taking the other eight places (7,960 patents granted).

But statistics alone cannot clearly show the legacy of R&D and diversification left by Dr Mitarai. A look at Canon's product groups, however, can. Canon today has six major product groups:

Office Imaging Products, Peripheral Products, Bubble Jet Products, Chemicals, Cameras, and Optical Products. Products now range from copiers, fax machines and scanners to the recent development, digital cameras. This last is the only product obviously directly descended from the cameras dreamed of in the 1930s, but every other product was developed as a result of Canon's expertise in imaging, as was Dr Mitarai's first X-ray camera. In fact, it wouldn't be too far from the truth to say that Canon is a one-product company. And that product is image.

Almost everything that Canon makes today is a result of the pioneering of Dr Mitarai, and, in line with his philosophy, almost everything made by Canon today has a value to society other than simply economic. Tomomasa Matsui, the retired managing director, is one of the few former Canon employees still to remember the early days of the company and the vital role played by Mitarai. Matsui joined Canon in 1942 after five years with silk-maker Shoei, a subsidiary of Fuji Bank and a company with close ties to Canon. There was at that time some talk of a merger between the two companies, and Matsui was transferred as an accountant to the camera manufacturer. He explains that he wasn't over-eager to make the change since in the early 1940s Canon was a very small company acting mainly as a subcontractor to the then largest optical products maker, Nikon, a member of the Mitsubishi *zaibatsu* (financial–industrial economic combine). The merger never occurred, and Matsui eventually came under the influence of Dr Mitarai and was soon his greatest fan and strongest supporter.

Says Matsui, 'It was impossible to separate Dr Mitarai from his medical practice even though he was running a company at the same time. Until the end of the war, he would come into the Canon office at around seven-thirty a.m. and work very hard, mainly encouraging people and raising morale, until eleven-thirty when he left for his clinic. The greatest gift he gave to Canon was his humanity and his judgment of people.

'Being an accountant, I didn't always understand what he was doing, and he would often have to remind me how to evaluate people. "When judging people," he would say, "you should go 50 per cent on the first look, when you can quickly see what is wrong with them, and the other 50 per cent of your judgment should come from questioning and seeing how they respond." This is a typical method of medical diagnosis which Dr Mitarai applied to business with almost unfailing success.

'He had the very rare ability to measure people up very quickly, and very often would overlook some negative traits because they were outweighed by a positive attitude or a required ability. It seems, however, that if he put his faith in someone who subsequently disappointed him, he could quite quickly amend his opinions. Fortunately this didn't happen very often.'

In 1945, after Japan's defeat, Mitarai's ability to judge personnel was severely tested. During the months leading up to Hiroshima and Nagasaki, the Japanese state and infrastructure had practically ceased to exist. There were shortages of almost everything, and the depression of impending defeat, though never admitted publicly, was sucking the determination from the people. Canon was no different from many other companies in that it kept struggling on, but many members of the work-force had given up and simply couldn't see the point of hard work. Absenteeism soared as workers took unofficial time off to search for food, clothing and anything else that was only available on the black market.

Once the American-led Occupation had begun to impose order again, however, companies had to start making new plans. Dr Mitarai believed that some Canon workers had taken un-necessary advantage of the wartime conditions to skimp on their commitment to the company, whilst others had continued to work hard and remain loyal despite terrible working and living conditions. He wanted to reward the loyal workers and get rid of the untrustworthy, so in August 1945 he dismissed all employees, with severance pay, and wound up the company.

In October of the same year, however, he re-formed Canon and hired a small number of the trusted former staff to get things moving again. Among the re-hired employees was Matsui, who had been one of the luckier members of Japan's Imperial Navy, having been called up only shortly before the war ended, and demobbed almost immediately.

Matsui explains: 'From the rubble and ashes of Tokyo it was hard to believe, in those early post-war years, that anything of any value could ever be rebuilt. But during his years at Hokkaido Imperial University, Dr Mitarai had been strongly influenced by the philosophy of the American scholar, William Clark.'

Clark, president of the Massachusetts Agricultural College, had, along with a team of other American educators, taught in an agricultural college in Hokkaido in 1875. During his stay in Hokkaido he had given instruction on modern agricultural practices and methods, as well as attempting strong indoctrination into Protestant Christianity. The attempt at conversion didn't really work, but, even today almost every Japanese remembers Clark for the typically American slogan he taught his students in Hokkaido: 'Boys, be ambitious!'

Though not a Christian, Mitarai had been impressed with Clark's beliefs and, throughout his life, always attempted to attain the highest goals possible, both on a personal level and for his company. Thus, in October 1945, a new Canon, smaller and perhaps wiser than the pre-war company, rose from the ashes of fascism and feudalism to a world of democracy and individual choice, much to the taste of Dr Takeshi Mitarai.

Ironically, the soldiers of the US forces that had brought Japan to its first-ever defeat in an international conflict, and reduced its industry to ashes, were to bring about a rapid change in Canon's fortunes. It must have been difficult for Mitarai to look on the future with anything but pessimism, but Clark's slogan was to bring him through the dark early post-war days. When he considered the economy of post-war Japan, it became clear to him that, for several years at least, the Occupation Forces were going to be the only people in the country with anything like a reasonable disposable income. And, he thought, what Japanese products did they buy with their dollars? After a little simple research he realized that just about the only Japanese-made products the Americans were taking home at the end of their tours of duty were pearls and silk. Why not, he thought, add an industrially produced product to the short list? And as cameras were still not taxed in Japan, he began to aim the marketing of Canon cameras at returning American GIs. The plan was extremely successful, to say the least. Production soared because of both official Occupation policy and non-official Occupation Force bargain-hunting.

It was obvious to General Douglas MacArthur, head of the Supreme Command Allied Powers (SCAP), upon his arrival in Tokyo, that Japan was in no position to pay for its own food and other necessities, let alone immediate war reparations. He had to come up with a plan to finance the Japanese economy in the short term with only minimal payments from Washington. One such plan would achieve the double goals of getting Japanese industry back on its feet and financing the bills for necessities by using Japanese industrial output as collateral for food imports from the United States and other countries.

Upon its re-establishment, therefore, Canon was ordered to deliver all its products to SCAP. Considering that during the war years camera production of ten units a month was considered high, the demands of SCAP were astronomic. In February 1946, for example, the Occupation ordered Canon to deliver 10,000 cameras by the end of June of the same year, a production of around 2,000 units a month. And this was only production to pay for national collateral.

There were also considerable sales made directly to the American Occupation market. According to *The Canon Handbook* (Canon Inc., 5th edition, 1994), 'Occupation US Army soldiers [were] eager to buy cameras and came directly to the Meguro head office plant by jeep.' This American-powered dramatic increase in output and, therefore, cash flow allowed Dr Mitarai to plan for the future with some optimism and, thanks to Clark, some ambition.

Once again, very much as at the start of the company before the war, Canon set itself extremely high targets. Almost immediately after the October 1945 re-start, Mitarai penned the new company slogan, again aiming at German superiority: 'Let's Catch Up and Pass Leica.' Though the slogan may seem to be pure propaganda aimed at encouraging the work-force, Mitarai also intended to make a different point.

Immediately after the war, some members of Canon wanted to improve cash flow by marketing a range of cheap and relatively low-quality cameras. This, they argued, would provide the breathing space necessary to organize the design and production of a high-quality range. Mitarai, however, was totally against this plan, saying, 'Once you have a name for low quality it is hard to shed that image. Canon must only make products that will enhance its image with the buyers and ensure our future with repeat sales.' He won the battle and low-quality Canon cameras never saw the light of day.

The final preliminary step towards the Canon of today came in September 1947 when the company's name was officially changed to Canon Camera Co., Inc. In yet another move away from typical Japanese tradition and conservatism, Dr Mitarai insisted that the company name be written in *katakana*, the phonetic Japanese alphabet used for foreign or imported words, instead of *hiragana*, the syllabary for true Japanese words. With this move Mitarai not only satisfied a desire for modernism, but gave ordinary Japanese the feeling that Canon was a producer of exotic, foreign equipment, not just another run-of-the-mill Japanese mass producer. And this was only the start of a modernization, rationalization and humanization process that continues at Canon today.

CHAPTER THREE

From the windows of Oita Canon Inc., Canon's subsidiary on the southern island of Kyushu, there is an unobscured view of all arrivals and departures at the tiny local domestic airfield. It can be a particularly useful prospect for people expecting visitors. During my meetings with a cross-section of the company's Kyushu-based staff, several employees told me that this view can give them a sometimes vital opportunity for a final wash and brush-up before a visiting VIP arrives at the plant. If such a visitor turns right from the terminal, he will soon be at the home of Canon's founder, Dr Takeshi Mitarai; but if he turns left, he is only ten minutes from the factory. Even so, landing at Oita is like arriving on another planet.

Oita Canon is just about as far from the image of a Japanese multinational as you can get. For non-Japanese arrivals, the feeling is one of alienation. The scenery visible from the lushly foliated hill where the factory is located, rolling down to a beautifully blue sea, is so typically Japanese that one inevitably feels a long, long way from home. This sense of strangeness was strengthened in my case, by the fact that the gate guard interrogated my Japanese companions in great detail, but only ever referred to me in the third person, in a does-he-take-sugar manner. However, as often in Japan, there is nothing you can do to get people to speak directly to you, and it was best merely to take lungfuls of some of the freshest air in Japan, and let my eyes wander above the palm trees from the sea, on my right, or to the mountains to my left. I did just that, and the air and scenery alone made the trip worthwhile, even before I'd managed to enter the factory.

Eventually the visitor will be let in and, if lucky, meet Hisayoshi Nozawa, president of Oita Canon. Nozawa is one of the many exceptions to the normal Japanese rule that Canon has chosen to employ. The opposite of the normally taciturn businessman, he welcomes visitors and questions equally. Asked why Canon chose Oita, he is absolutely candid. 'Dr Mitarai, one of the founders of the company, came from here, and though he went to university in Hokkaido, before working in Tokyo, the family has continued its close contacts with the area. There is also the fact that Oita prefecture Governor Morihiko Hiramatsu has been actively encouraging high-tech investment under the slogan "One product for one village". But don't think that Canon's location here is purely because of family ties. Texas Instruments is less than thirty kilometres [nineteen miles] away and you can get to Toshiba's semiconductor plant and Sony's factory in about thirty minutes by car.

'There was a problem with low population. In fact, it would be better to describe it as under-population. There was no industry, so young people were moving out of the area to get jobs. The Governor decided to try to arrest the drain, and Canon, of course, was willing to help.'

Nozawa is proud of Oita Canon's development. 'Of 1,200 employees today, 100 come from other Canon facilities. All the others, with the exception of non-Japanese trainees, have been hired locally. And it has been a success. My motto,' he continues, 'is "Assimilate Locally", and with this in mind, I even joined the local over-forties baseball team.'

This intention to fit in with local society, even on a global scale, is typical of Canon. Western visitors to Japan are often shocked to discover that the Japanese, long thought to be some of the cleanest and most fastidious people in the world, can survive in a country where public toilets are always filthy. After a short stay, however, most non-Japanese recognize the crucial distinction in Japanese society between private and public. 'Private' means that someone recognizable has responsibility, therefore everything is pristine. 'Public' means that there is no individual responsibility, so who cares?

In most cases in Japan, this private/public stance is taken a step further. 'Private' means what the Japanese want or expect, so everything is done along mutually agreed lines. 'Public' is what the world as a whole expects, so is of little domestic importance. Japan, basically, doesn't care what the world thinks of it on a domestic level. The last thing most Japanese give a hoot about is whether or not the rest of the world understands them. After all, understanding would destroy the national myth of uniqueness.

Most Japanese, individuals and corporations, will gladly explain the generally accepted reasons for Japan's post-war success to anybody willing to listen. The whole thing, they will say, is due to the inherited Japanese willingness to work hard and cooperate with each other, combined with the lifetime employment system. No mention will ever be made of the millions of dollars pumped into the Japanese economy through the post-war American Marshall Plan. Nor will anyone admit that first the Korean and then the Vietnam War, with America's dependence on Japan for Rest and Recreation as well as cheap military supplies, had anything to do with Japan's industrial resurgence. Canon, on the other hand, is proof of what really happened.

The lessons of Dr Takeshi Mitarai's life are well worth the study. Doctors in Japan are almost always held in high esteem and, no matter how bad, treated with politeness. Only in recent years have the Japanese begun to mistrust their doctors along the lines they have previously reserved for politicians, often said to be the lowest of the low. In 1996, for example, it surprised many Japanese that Dr Takeshi Abe, head of the government's AIDS research department, was charged with the illegal deaths of many haemophiliacs after admitting that the government failed to notify health carers of the danger of treating people with unheated blood products.

In the past, a doctorate in medicine was merely thought of as a licence to print money. There simply wasn't a requirement to help improve society. In this way, as in many others, Dr Mitarai proved to be different. First and foremost, Takeshi Mitarai was a medical doctor as understood by the West. As Louis Kraar puts it in his and Seiichi Takikawa's book, *Japanese Maverick* (John Wiley & Sons, 1994), 'A physician with limited business experience, Dr Takeshi Mitarai led Canon's dazzling post-war growth almost by accident. He bankrolled the original Precision Optical Research Instruments Laboratory and was eventually drawn more into management.'

Mitarai himself admitted that he hadn't originally intended to be a businessman. In Kraar's book he explains why he got involved with the fledgling company. 'At that time, it was only seven or eight years after my graduation from medical school, where even the microscopes that we used were made in Germany. So I thought this kind of business was right for Japan.' There was also the fact that he knew and liked the people he was getting involved with. 'It was a kind of comrade-like relationship. To register a company at that time, you needed seven organizers, and we were all good friends.'

For the first few years of his relationship with Canon, Mitarai remained purely an adviser and financial backer. Despite a brief period at the reins during the war, it was only really after the company was re-formed in 1945 that he was able to begin instigating his unusual plans for future development.

In those early years Dr Mitarai showed his true colours. Tomomasa Matsui, the retired former managing director who joined the company in 1942, says, 'Dr Mitarai had a phenomenal ability to measure people up and choose the right ones. He knew how to judge and bring harmony even to disparate groups; perhaps this was something he'd learnt as the head of his dormitory at Hokkaido University.'

Almost immediately after the war, Mitarai began to use his judgment to choose the most reliable workers and meld them into a team, the pattern of which it is still possible to see in the Canon of today. The company nurtured by Mitarai was very strongly Japanese, in that slogans and philosophies were handed down for the workers to uphold, but also took the best of what the West could offer, as in its revolutionary post-war labour practices. The Japanese need to work in teams and feel they belong to various groups, from the family at the smallest level, through the project team and the company at the middle level, to the nation on the grandest scale. In order to achieve this sense of belonging, easily recognized and simply remembered codes of behaviour must be available. Thus almost every Japanese company has a collection of slogans and philosophies that evolve with the organization's successes or failures.

One of the earliest examples of sloganry at Canon was the pre-war catch-phrase, 'Let's Beat Leica'. Not very sophisticated, perhaps, but definitely something that every single worker could understand and attempt to achieve. After the war, however, the philosophies that have made Canon what it is today really began to take shape. Even as the company prepares for the change of the millennium, it can be safely said that underlying each of the company's manufacturing and business operations is a philosophy. This is expressed in a corporate purpose deeply ingrained in the minds of Canon's Japanese employees. Non-Japanese employees, though aware of the corporate philosophy, tend to be a little bit more pragmatic about acceptance of commandments from above. In a 1979 interview Dr Mitarai explained, 'Canon's corporate purpose commits the company to strive for the very best in every product and activity, and thereby contribute to society. This purpose has continued unchanged for forty-two years despite enormous changes in the company and its business environment. It is the backbone of our entire multinational corporate complex.

'In day-to-day business, we ask our employees to take pride in their work, and to perform each task responsibly. This is equally true from manufacturing through to international service and marketing.

'In 1940 Canon produced an indirect X-ray camera, Japan's first, and it had a dramatic effect in reducing tuberculosis throughout the country. In 1965 an X-ray camera for the stomach, the Magen Mirror Camera, was introduced, and proved particularly useful in early diagnosis of stomach cancer. In 1976 Canon introduced the non-mydriatic retinal camera which permits examinations and diagnosis through the eyes, often called the body's windows. In this way, and in many others, we have contributed not only to Canon, but to society as a whole.'

It is interesting that at a time when practically every other Japanese company had only one aim – survival – the president of Canon, one of its founders, was considering how his company could contribute to society. This really does sound more like a doctor's approach than a businessman's. In *Japanese Maverick*, Seiichi Takikawa explains: 'It was really simple to work for Dr Mitarai. After all, he was an MD and didn't know the details of business practices. He would leave them to you. When you are trusted so much, you just have to do a job well.'

Thus Dr Mitarai selected his employees carefully. He chose bright young men to run the company, including current Chairman Ryuzaburo Kaku and Canon Sales Co. Chairman Seiichi Takikawa. Once he had his new recruits in place, he was able to concentrate on the policies and philosophies that would distinguish Canon from most other companies. The most basic of these, handed down very early in the company's history, is called the Three Js – *ji-hatsu, ji-kaku* and *ji-chi* (self-motivation, self-awareness and self-management).

Canon's personnel policies are based on the conviction that a worker's participation in the company must be consistent with, and contributory to, his or her family responsibilities. The harmony of the company, its members and their family members is essential to the well-being of all. This is not to say that Canon's attitude is paternalistic in the usual sense. Rather, as in the company's Three Js policy, the stress is on responsibility and awareness of the work community's basic goals. Every aspect of Canon's personnel administration is intended to reinforce the three qualities of self-motivation, self-awareness and self-management. In his 1979 interview, Dr Mitarai explained: 'The essential meaning is that one should work responsibly, and be aware of the group's goals. This is particularly important in teamwork situations.'

Canon's personnel policies certainly differ from those of most other Japanese corporations, and have done so from the company's earliest years. One of the first moves that placed Canon apart from other Japanese companies is nowadays recognized as a typical facet of Japanese-style management. It concerns the equality of workers.

Prior to June 1943, workers at Canon had been categorized by function. Administration and office workers were considered full employees and were salaried. Factory employees, on the other hand, were on a daily or weekly payment system. This was further complicated by a wage formula that included basic pay plus additions for skill level, length of service and, in some cases, piece-work.

The distinction between the two types of employee was shown even more clearly in an almost British way. Until 1943, office employees and factory workers were required to enter the company through different gates. What is now thought of as the

Japanese-style all–one–family system simply did not exist and, as in many industrial concerns throughout the world, there was a very clear 'us and them' mentality.

Dr Mitarai proposed to change all this by making every employee a member of the Canon family. On 24 March 1943 he presented the board of directors with his proposals. All employees, whether clerical or manual, were to be regarded as regular employees, *sha-in* in Japanese, and there was to be a pan-company salary scale based on length of service and skill levels, which would be tested on an annual basis. Ironically, some manual employees, potentially the largest beneficiaries of Dr Mitarai's plan, thought this was merely a clever way to reduce their wages, and the company witnessed a small but significant exodus of experienced workers. Within a few months, however, the Japanized Western merit system was instigated, and workers of all skills were not simply made equals financially, but were told to enter and leave the company by the main gate. Dr Mitarai explained further in his 1979 interview: 'Under Canon's policy of putting the right person in the right job employees are rewarded for their abilities instead of being promoted because of personal contacts, or simply because of seniority. This reflects a unique combination of traditional Japanese lifetime employment with the Western merit promotion system.

'For example,' he continued, 'all sub-managerial employees take annual examinations to test their proficiency in various aspects of their individual jobs. And then, even if a higher position is not immediately open, a passing score in the tests automatically brings a salary increase to reward the achievement. This objective testing system makes promotion much more open than in the traditional Japanese system.'

This may be a better system than that employed by many companies, but even today some members of Canon's staff are not convinced that it is truly fair (see Chapter Six). But it must be said that getting over the hurdle caused by a system of extreme prejudice was one of the major contributions Dr Mitarai bequeathed to the company.

Another stumbling-block often faced by Japanese companies, particularly as they try to expand their overseas operations, is how to treat non-Japanese. In this area, at least, Canon seems to be very much an exception, and a possible model for other Japanese multinationals. There are many examples. Several non-Japanese subsidiaries are now headed and mainly staffed by locals, with hardly a Japanese head to be seen. And the plans for local globalization, as Canon calls it, are moving along apace. President Fujio Mitarai, himself a twenty-three-year US resident, even goes as far as to say, 'It is not a question of if Canon will ever select a non-Japanese board member, but when!' Even down at basic levels there is a willingness to internationalize that is not evidenced in many other Japanese companies. In Oita Canon in Kyushu, for example, there is a specific programme to train Malaysians through on-the-job experience. The trainees will eventually return to Malaysia and, it is hoped, play key roles in Canon's Asian growth. Before starting the programme, Canon looked carefully at what the trainees would need and, amongst other things, realized that religious and cultural norms in Malaysia demanded different toilet facilities. So, throughout the factory, visitors now see signs that read 'Malaysian Toilet'. When internationalization is taken to this extreme there is hope for the future.

All too often in many Japanese companies, the only people who get to the top are Japanese and occasional Caucasians, but Canon seems genuinely interested in training local people to run local subsidiaries and affiliates, irrespective of the colour of their skin. There is a definite attempt to bring about equality.

Alongside Dr Takeshi Mitarai's Three Js philosophy and his

demand for the equal treatment of all employees, is his New Family policy. According to Dr Mitarai, 'Canon is a company for all of us – it is not just for the benefit of a select few. It is essential that we share a sense of satisfaction in our work and dedication to the tasks set before us.'

He continues to explain how a Japanese company differs from a Western company in the same way that an employee in Japan differs from an employee in the West. 'The English word "employee" does not truly describe the Japanese situation. Our word, *sha-in*, is better translated as "member of the firm". There is a feeling of mutual responsibility in the fact that we do not fire employees when times are hard, but instead we ask them to share the burden with us. I am very proud that we have never had a strike at any Canon facility in Japan.' Considering that Canon was one of the first Japanese companies to be unionized, almost immediately after the war, in July 1946, the fact that it has never suffered a strike in its home country is noteworthy, even for a Japanese company. Once again, the hand of Dr Mitarai can be seen in the structuring of the relatively strifeless company.

In the West, union membership is normally horizontal and dependent on job description. Electricians, for example, belong to the same union although they may work for many different companies. In Japan, on the contrary, unions are usually vertical. Union members are employees of the same company. Thus a strike by a Japanese union will generally affect only a single company, not a complete industry. However, there are trade union organizations, much like the TUC in Britain, to which individual company unions belong, thereby achieving at least the appearance of national power. In reality, however, these national organizations are nothing more than fund-raising and support groups for politicians. And this is where Canon, yet again, moves apart from the crowd. As a company, Canon makes no political donations whatsoever, preferring instead to remain totally independent of the political system. Likewise, Canon Workers' Union (CWU) remains politically unaffiliated and deals only with the management of the company on matters of business. Membership is open to all blue- and white-collar workers up to the *kacho-dairi* (deputy manager) level, and is regarded not as a show of independence from management but as another sign of company membership.

When the union was first organized in 1946, Dr Mitarai made it clear that it would be seen as a partner in corporate management, not as an opponent. And this philosophy continues to this day. Any interviewer trying to get statements of independent policy from CWU organizers is truly wasting his time. 'Everything,' he will be told by union executives, 'is on the table for discussion between the CWU and corporate management. And because of this policy of cooperation and coexistence, we are extremely proud to say there has never been a strike at Canon.'

In fact, if the interviewer closed his eyes and just listened to the words, it would be very difficult to tell whether the speaker was a union leader or a member of the board of directors, so similar are the responses. But this doesn't mean that the CWU is a mere lapdog. The fact that there do not appear to be any areas of major strife is due in main to the hard work and long hours spent by management and union discussing just about every aspect of Canon's operations. Even in a land built on consensus, the relationship between CWU and corporate management is unusual. There really don't appear to be any areas that the two can't or don't discuss. Often, management does not get all it wants, but just as often CWU has to compromise, so in the long term everybody is happy.

Almost from its inception, CWU has played an important and constructive role in Canon's development. In 1946, managing director Tomomasa Matsui, now retired, was one of the union leaders. He explains what happened. 'We and the board, under

Dr Mitarai, had agreed on the monthly salary levels, but I decided that it was my role to convince him of the necessity of an incentive system as well. After we had talked, it was obvious that Dr Mitarai saw the sense of such a system, and, under the slogan "High Productivity, High Wages", we decided to go ahead. This not only had the advantage of encouraging those already employed by Canon to work harder, but also gave us the edge on recruitment, and enabled us to get the best of the recently demobbed engineers and researchers. This openness to discussion has long been a vital part of the relationship between management and the union, and has certainly been a major contributor to corporate growth.'

Dr Mitarai, it seems, would on the whole be pleased with the way his company is developing, at least in personnel matters. But, warns business journalist Toru Arai of *Nikkan Kogyo Shimbun*, now is no time to relax. 'The people at the top have very strong personalities, but the younger, middle management don't, and, in fact, appear a little wishy-washy. This is probably due to the rapid growth Canon has experienced during its relatively short life, particularly since the end of the war.

'When Canon was small, the employees, and many of them are still there in top management, were hungry. They were willing to fight for success and do anything to achieve growth. But nowadays the company is big, somewhat stodgier than it used to be, and all middle management is interested in doing is to pass the company on to the next generation without making any spectacular mistakes. In a way Canon can be seen as a microcosm of Japan as a whole.

'Canon is an evolutionary rather than a revolutionary company. It has thoughtfully and steadily been meeting the needs of industry, society in general, and its employees for many years. However, I don't feel that there is currently a system that necessarily brings the most brilliant people to the top. There are definite signs of stagnation. That said, however, Canon does have a remarkable track record of introducing completely new systems and philosophies to deal with problems as they arise, so it's very possible that they will rise to the occasion and an answer will be found.'

Despite this quibble, there seems little doubt that Dr Takeshi Mitarai left a sound and strong company to his successors. More importantly, perhaps, his humanist philosophy has instilled a spirit in Canon that may well make it unique among Japanese multinationals, and be eagerly passed from management generation to management generation.

Dr Mitarai probably explains the Canon way better than anyone else could. In his 1979 New Year's Address to company employees he said, 'We must recognize that credibility is essential to all our activities. Trust comes from a daily practice: never telling lies and never deceiving others.

'Within the next few years I would like to strengthen Canon's reputation as a company to be trusted, in Japan and throughout the world, inside and outside the organization. This will make Canon truly worthy of respect, and will enhance our future growth and expansion.

'To sum up,' continued Dr Mitarai, 'the spirit is the most important part of the company. If the heart is good, business will be good. I wanted to build a company which actually achieves its ideals, and I'm proud of the distance Canon has covered in that respect.

'A single man can't win the struggle all by himself, but if tens of thousands of Canon family members all understand the company's aims and we put our strength together, we will achieve our mutual goals.'

Canon may not yet have achieved all Dr Mitarai's goals, but, under the leadership of current President Fujio Mitarai and Chairman Ryuzaburo Kaku, the game is still being played, and the rules remain the same.

CHAPTER FOUR

'During my childhood, I suffered very badly from shyness and was always blushing. One evening I overheard my parents discussing me, and I'll always remember what my father said on the subject. He told my mother, "It is a virtue of the Japanese that they realize what shame is. There is nothing wrong with blushing in front of other people." That evening, I think I learned one of the most important lessons of my life, and to this day I try to live by a creed of facing shame if deserved, while, of course, trying to maintain ethical personal and corporate standards that will obviate any cause for shame.' So says Ryuzaburo Kaku, chairman of Canon Inc., the rebel philosopher and, some say, conscience of Japanese business. Kaku's philosophy of life and business is not what is generally expected from a senior Japanese businessman, but this is hardly surprising. Much of his childhood was spent in straitened circumstances in China as well as Japan. A child of the global depression, being born in 1926, and of war, living through both the Sino-Japanese and the Second World Wars, and with the truly humbling experience of surviving the Nagasaki atom bombing, he lacks the self-assuredness verging on arrogance of many of Japan's pampered, semi-aristocratic, old-school-tie type of leader.

Though born in Aichi prefecture and brought up in Kyushu, Kaku's first real memories are of Shinjuku, nowadays called Tokyo's Manhattan because of its skyscraper skyline, but which, in the days of the Depression, was 'ironically full of people with nowhere to shelter for the night and empty homes that nobody could afford to rent, and where in a tiny two-storey house lived my parents, two older brothers, and myself, all trying to survive on what my father brought home. Though a scholarly type – good at calligraphy and Chinese classics – he unfortunately had an innate inability to conform to the dictates of common sense.'

Masamitsu Tadenuma, who joined Canon in 1954, in the same intake as Kaku, and eventually retired in 1994 as Kaku's executive assistant, puts things a little more kindly, describing Kaku senior as 'Unusual. The kind of man who has no material desires. He loved China very much and had many true Chinese friends. Kaku-san was influenced very much by his father, from whom he learned his far-sightedness and his selfless love for all human beings.'

After struggling for years in Tokyo, Kaku's father was offered a job with a newspaper in Shanghai, whereupon the entire family upped sticks and arrived in China, ominously only slightly before the outbreak of the Sino-Japanese War. His life in China, the Chinese philosophy, and particularly the attitudes of Japanese expatriates in the country have all left their marks on Kaku's personality and have helped to shape both his personal and business philosophies.

One particular lesson was learned very painfully. This concerned the value of the individual, and taught the young Kaku not to look down on people, both literally and metaphorically. One late afternoon he was leaning over the second-floor balcony of his parents' house when he saw a Chinese pedlar passing by. Being a young, rather spoilt expatriate brat, and having no respect for such peasants, he decided to tease the hawker and started to call him names. An argument soon ensued, and the insults tossed between the two grew ruder and more personal. In an attempt to outshout the Chinaman and at the same time assert his superiority, the young Kaku leaned further over the balcony than he should have and fell suddenly to the ground, injuring his shoulder in the process. Nowadays, Kaku teaches that all people should be treated with dignity, and that arrogance is generally the result of ignorance. It is the taunters of the world who are really lacking moral fibre and dignity, not those who are simply struggling to survive.

Survival in today's technical business world may seem a million miles away from life in pre-war Shanghai, but Canon's current commitment, not only to research and development, but to the commercializing of that research, may also be traced to the China of sixty years ago. Kaku's father, unlike most Japanese, couldn't seem to stick at one job. Even after moving to China, he didn't remain in a single position. At different times he worked on a newspaper, was a director of a publishing firm, and acted as an adviser to a leading Chinese figure. His work may not have been lucrative, but it gave the family status, and their home was often filled with noisy Japanese expatriates playing mah-jongg and drinking heavily.

According to Kaku, a teetotaller, 'I got used to the noisiness of mah-jongg, but never to the outrageousness of drunken men.' However, one lesson, the results of which can be seen at Canon on a daily basis, did come from one of these gatherings. A drunken but still philosophical Japanese berated Kaku's two elder brothers, who had both been getting extraordinarily good grades at high school, by saying, 'You should never be number one in your class, because then you are studying purely for the sake of studying. Be second or even a little below and the chances are that you are studying to learn. If you study just for the sake of grades, you will inevitably end up narrow-minded and unable to see the wood for the trees.'

At Canon today, both in the global research centres and throughout the rest of the company, this spirit is fundamental to company philosophy. Canon spends a higher percentage of turnover on research than most of its Japanese or foreign competitors. Unlike many of them, however, both the research into and the commercialization of new products must not simply be seen as a race to get something 'better' out before the competition. Each projected new product must satisfy criteria regarding how it will alter the lives of consumers, the ecology of the world and the profitability of the company. Simply being top of the class is not Canon's aim; learning lessons on a global basis and putting them into practice is. On a personal basis, Kaku says, 'I don't think I could ever be said to have disappointed my father's friend. I have always been what is probably best described as an honourable student. I was never top of the class, and even failed my university entrance examinations the first two times. So it can't be said that I ever studied for studying's sake.'

Kaku's belief that all people should be treated equally and with dignity derives not only from his experiences in China, but also from seeing the Japanese as outsiders. The sheer clannishness of most Japanese makes it impossible for many of them even to understand what non-Japanese feel, with the result that their relationships with *gaijin* tend to be tainted by either condescension or jealousy: condescension to almost all Asians and developing nations, and jealousy towards anyone better off in general and the white nations in particular. Because of this, other Asians often refer to the Japanese as 'bananas' – yellow on the outside but white on the inside.

Few Japanese ever experience what it is like to be an outsider dealing with the Japanese, and, therefore, even fewer can ever deal with non-Japanese on a basis of understanding and equality. Kaku, however, understands very well the feeling of being an outsider. In 1936, as the war in China escalated, his father was asked to move to Chingtao to take up a part-time appointment in the Japanese Consulate. In just over twelve months, however, the political and military situations went from bad to worse, and his family chose to go back to Kyushu, while he remained in Chingtao continuing his diplomatic role alone, until conditions should improve.

When Kaku was enrolled in the local school back in Kyushu, for the first time in his life he was bullied. He had unwittingly committed what were regarded as the two cardinal sins in fascist Japan; he was an outsider, having come from China, and a figure of envy, his ancestors having run a sake brewery and built a castle in the town. Today Kaku explains that he was deeply shocked and that this was when he began to realize that the Japanese could be frighteningly unkind and blind to common decencies, particularly if the target was seen as an outsider and thus beneath contempt. This was something he had never suspected while living a relatively protected life in China. As a result of this experience, Kaku insists that Canon today tries in every way and in every country to offer the same levels of human dignity to all its employees, partners and customers.

After learning this valuable lesson in Japan, in 1938 the young Kaku was happy to be able to return with his family to live again with his father in China, the political situation having stabilized. He stayed there until it was time for him to return yet again to Japan to attend senior high school and prepare for university. During this period in China, he claims he learned a great deal about dignity under duress. Once again, his father is cited as the major influence on his development. 'My father gave me a copy of *The Count of Monte Cristo*, and for the first time in my life I realized that strong people can emerge from suffering with dignity.'

From then on Kaku has always loved reading, devouring thousands upon thousands of volumes, not only of literature, but also of philosophy, from which he has distilled his own unique, almost pacifistic attitude to life.

The most obvious aspect of Chairman Kaku's personal philosophy is his belief in the dignity of the individual and the lessons to be learned from China, the world's longest-surviving civilization and the sleeping giant of Asia. 'Of my recent readings,' he says, 'the book that has impressed me most was *Wild Swans – Three Daughters of China* by Jung Chang. Since I read this book my opinion of China has been modified. Remembering the China of the thirties, and reading reports of the country under communism, I had tended to see the country as a mire of corruption and bribery. But when I read of the sufferings of the writer's father, a communist official who struggled against the bland and corrupted uniformity of the Cultural Revolution, I realized that even within a despotic administration, purity can be found. In him I saw the reflection of my own father, and saw, yet again, the necessity of individual dignity as opposed to mass conformity.'

In the Japan of today, alas, Chairman Kaku claims that all he can see is a populace of conformity led by an exclusive clique, differing only in political bent from the Chinese communists of the Cultural Revolution of the 1960s. The Japanese bureaucracy, arguably the country's most powerful clique, and most large Japanese companies operate a *gakubatsu* (old school-tie) system, whereby many of the employees, and certainly most of those who actually run the company, are graduates of the same university. In a country where people often claim a lack of understanding of the British-style class system, it is interesting to note that the *Todai-Kyodai* (Tokyo University–Kyoto University, the Japanese equivalent of Oxbridge) clique practically run the country, without, apparently, anyone ever realizing this is a class system in the purest form.

The only Japanese definition of a class system is one run by aristocrats for the benefit of aristocrats, and since General MacArthur and the American Occupation did away with Japan's peerage, it stands to reason, the Japanese believe, that no such system can exist. The simple fact that who you are and what you are in Japan is almost totally dependent on who your father was, where you are from, and where you went to university doesn't appear to strike the Japanese as a class system. So most major companies are happy to employ on an it's-not-what-you-know-but-who-you-know basis – with the exception of Canon, that is.

Canon's policy of hiring the most qualified person for the job has been enshrined in the company's unwritten laws since its founding, and has certainly been strengthened by the personal experiences of Chairman Kaku. From 1939 to 1944, the height of Japan's militarist period, Kaku was in junior high school in Chingtao, where he was appointed company commander in the school cadet force.

Despite feeling that upon this appointment he 'became more aggressive', Kaku admits that on hearing of the 8 December 1941 attack on Pearl Harbor, he felt 'very nervous'. This, combined with overhearing his father and his associates discussing the Mao Zedong-led Long March did not inspire him with optimism for Japan's short-term future. However, he was young and Japanese, so there was really no choice but to be patriotic.

In Kaku's own words: 'As I was deeply involved with my school's military training and was young and fit, I decided to apply for a commission in the Imperial Navy. During the interview the officer questioning me asked about my relationship to a certain person, who turned out to be my uncle, with whom the interviewer was well acquainted. To my disgust I was turned down for the Navy, and could not help but come to the conclusion that the interviewer refused me purely because he did not want to be responsible for sending the nephew of his friend to his death in the war. This was when I lost faith in the military, a belief that stays with me to today.'

When Kaku was sent back to high school in Japan, he ostensibly studied science, but in reality spent most of his time playing rugby and discovering the philosophies of Kant and Goethe. But this was brought to an end when, with Japan on the verge of defeat throughout the Pacific, and the entire war effort suffering

1 The office of Canon's predecessor, Seiki Kogaku Kenkyusho (Precision Optical Instruments Laboratory), established in Roppongi, Tokyo in 1933 to conduct research into quality cameras.

2 The Kwanon camera mark. The name came from the Buddhist Goddess of Mercy, Kannon, who is said to bring about benefits in this world. The lenses were named Kasyapa after Mahakasyapa, who was Buddha's disciple.

3 The Kwanon, Japan's first 35mm focal-plane-shutter camera, was produced in prototype form in 1934. The octagonal body shape was a unique design and became a model for the other Canon cameras in later years.

4 In 1951 Dr Takeshi Mitarai (president, 1942–74; chairman, 1974–84), *seated centre*, signed a contract with Jardine Matheson & Co. in Hong Kong for the exclusive distribution of all Canon products worldwide. With this, Canon's international marketing began.

5 Dr Takeshi Mitarai, *centre right*, and Takeo Maeda (president 1974–77), *centre left*, enjoy a three-legged race at the Sports Day in the mid-1950s.

6 The expatriates in the New York branch office, opened in 1955, the year Canon began its own launch into the overseas market.

7 The Canon booth at the Photokina Show in Cologne, Germany (1960). Photokina has a long history – since 1950 – as an international camera show. Canon had exhibited since 1956, but it was not until 1960 that it had a stand of its own. In 1970, Dr Takeshi Mitarai became the first Japanese to receive the Photokina Pin, an award given to those who have made a significant contribution to the industry.

8 President Takeshi Mitarai watches as the first Canonet camera is ceremoniously transported on its way to the domestic market from the Shimomaruko plant in 1961. Canonet was the first mass-produced lens-shutter-type electric eye (EE) camera. With the price kept at a reasonable level, this camera became an everyday consumer product, making the dream of 'one family, one camera' a reality.

9 Canonets being assembled at the Toride plant in 1961. As the Shimomaruko plant could no longer cope with the influx of orders for Canonets, a new assembly line was set up in haste at Toride in Ibaragi prefecture.

10 Dr Takeshi Mitarai shaking hands with Chairman Percy of the Bell & Howell Company in 1962. In 1961, Canon signed a contract with Bell & Howell, which became the exclusive camera distributor for North America. The partnership lasted from 1961 until 1972.

11 The ceremony in Panama (1967) to mark the first foundations of Canon Latin America, Inc., which was established as a sales company for South America. George Lewbel, president of Canon Latin America, is digging. Third from the right is Dr Takeshi Mitarai.

12 The Canola 130, the world's first ten-key electronic calculator, was introduced in 1964 and was a popular attraction at business shows.

13 Dr Takeshi Mitarai attending the 1968 opening ceremony of Canon Amsterdam N.V. (today, Canon Europa). Sitting next to him on the right is Masaaki Kobayashi, president of Canon Amsterdam N.V.

14 HRH Queen Elizabeth II on a tour of the Shimomaruko plant in 1975 with Dr Takeshi Mitarai, *left*, and Takeo Maeda (president, 1974-77).

15 President Takeo Maeda tells the Canon workforce about the Premier Company Plan at the New Year assembly in 1976. A committee was established to discuss development of production and sales systems.

16 A crowd gathering to take a look at the AE-1, the world's first computerized single-lens reflex camera, introduced in 1976.

from a serious shortage of labour, he was ordered, along with his classmates, to work in the shipyards of Nagasaki.

Kaku's war ended in only the second atomic explosion ever to occur as an act of war. 'On 9 August 1945, due to a shortage of materials, I had nothing to do, and so I settled down for a nap. Just as I rested my head on a table to sleep, I felt a burning sensation on my face, followed by the rushing and howling of a strong, overheated wind. Everything was thrown about, and shattered glass was everywhere. In panic I jumped from the window of the second floor, where I had been about to sleep, and ran into hiding.

'When I had had time to reflect on what had happened, putting to use my knowledge of physics and also what I had heard about secret research into a new doomsday weapon in Japan, I could only conclude that the explosion I had just survived was the result of an atomic bombing.

'I wasn't sure exactly what the effects of an atom bombing would be, but I realized that even those who, like me, had survived the initial explosion were still in a very dangerous position. I knew that on the site of the shipyard was an underground tunnel, where we had started to excavate an underground factory in order to survive conventional Allied bombing. I took all my fellow students to this tunnel and insisted that we all stayed below ground for as long as possible. Some of them, perhaps like the majority of Nagasaki citizens, had no idea of what had happened, and wanted to go back to the surface to have a look around, but I made everyone stay below, where we remained for a few hours. We lost many friends in the atomic bombing, but all fifteen of us who stayed underground are still alive.

'We then went back to our dormitory, which was in the suburbs of Nagasaki over the mountains from the bay and the shipyard. I was able to convince the group to stay there for three days, although some of my most conscientious colleagues suggested that we should report back to work as early as the following day. Once we were back in the shipyards, the manager told us to start clearing the site of a former foundry and, together with Dutch and British prisoners of war, we set about the task with little enthusiasm.

'Later that day, there was a sudden flash followed by a loud bang, and we all hit the dirt, thinking it was another bomb. Eventually we realized it had been a flash of lightning followed by a clap of thunder, a totally natural occurrence. As we scrambled embarrassed to our feet, we noticed a British officer emerging completely soaked from a pool of water in which he'd been totally submerged, and concluded that if it really had been another bomb, he'd probably have been the only survivor. Survival at this point had become merely a matter of who moved the fastest. There was no advantage in being a member of a so-called master race or, in fact, any race or religion. People were all the same when faced with identical circumstances.'

Even before this experience, during the war itself Kaku had begun to doubt the direction Japan was taking. 'We had been told that Japan was superior, and had been educated to believe that Japan could never lose. But when we went to see factories, we looked at lines and lines of machinery idle because of a lack of spare parts from abroad. It was then that the first understanding of the importance of a system of global partnerships began to come to me. Japan could not, and, perhaps more importantly, should not, stand alone.'

Becoming a member of global society on national, corporate and personal levels forms the basis of Kaku's philosophy. He believes that only through such partnerships can the world be saved from war, starvation, pollution and moral decadence. But he believes in the particular importance of personal commitment and responsibility. If you believe in something, he says, do not give in and do the wrong thing simply for the sake of conformity.

Unlike many Japanese, Kaku does not worship the glorious failures of his nation's history. Before Pearl Harbor, when the Japanese government was discussing the possibility of war with America, Admiral Yamamoto spoke out in clear opposition to the commencement of hostilities, saying that Japan could not win. However, he was overruled, and as a military officer did what he was ordered and led Japan into war. Most Japanese consider Yamamoto to be a hero because he did his duty despite his personal feelings. Kaku, however, feels that he was a disgrace to humanity. 'At the end of the war that he had initially opposed and then, in a complete dismissal of his beliefs, had led, Yamamoto should have committed suicide. He did not stand up for what he believed in and should not, therefore, be worshipped, even respected. Honour is what matters in life. Honour!'

This belief in honour and human dignity is the touchstone of Kaku's and Canon's *kyosei* philosophy. Kaku believes that unless all people work together for the common good, only disaster can result. 'Even as a survivor of the atomic bombing in Nagasaki, I cannot share the motives of the so-called "popular" demonstrations against the nuclear bombings. If Japan had had the bomb first, do you really believe it wouldn't have used it? The politicians and military leaders of the time wouldn't have hesitated for a second to use atomic weapons. However, personally, I am totally against making or using nuclear bombs, which can only bring disaster to the human race.'

Chairman Kaku is no less severe in his disdain for today's Japanese politicians and bureaucrats, basically condemning them all as spineless self-servers. He believes that little can be done with, or expected of, the existing generation of governmental leaders. In a typically unselfconscious and non-conforming Kaku move, he has recently started to invite himself to various universities, whose deans are usually too much in awe of the powerful businessman to refuse him, where he harangues the authorities and tells the students that it is up to them to change Japan.

Kaku explains: 'After failing for years to influence Japanese politicians, I have decided to change the target of my attack to the younger generation of college students, since I can feel their frustration at living in a society that won't even change an unjust system. What I am trying to do is to make as many speeches as possible to college students in an attempt to get my ideas over. I've given up expecting rapid change, and, even at my age, I am willing to wait another twenty years if necessary, until the students I am addressing today are actually running the country.

'I tell them that only by instigating a system of individual responsibility and acting morally and ethically can Japan escape from the quagmire of political, bureaucratic and business corruption in which it currently wallows.'

Kaku even goes so far as to blame his own generation, saying, 'Be very wary of trusting a Japanese businessman or politician over forty. He has already suffered enough as a young man in the corrupt system and is now reaping the rewards of seniority. It is just not in his interests to change, even slightly, the benefits of the status quo.'

At Canon this distrust and dislike of politicians and bureaucrats is carried to an extreme unusual in the normally consensus-forming and non-confrontational world of Japanese business. Unlike almost all major Japanese companies, Canon makes no donations to any political party and eschews contacts with the bureaucracy. In a way, this works against the company as it can hardly expect to get its share of a governmental pie after it has publicly declared it to be tainted with the poison of graft.

Although most of the company's employees are proud of this independent stance, it is, however, sometimes seen by younger members of staff as cutting off the nose to spite the face. Three male employees in their thirties, and representative of their age, expressed differing opinions on the subject of political contributions, showing the argument is not cut and dried. The first interviewee expressed pride in Canon's individualism, saying, 'We do business by ourselves without asking favours from politicians or bureaucrats, so it doesn't make any difference if we make political contributions or not.' The second man was a little more cynical. 'Even if you give political donations for the best reasons, they'll probably end up in some slush fund or other. If you could be sure of what your money was being used for, I could justify donating something to political parties; but in this country, you never will know what it is being used for!' The third interviewee, however, probably represented the most pragmatic view, and one that would be unlikely to appeal to Chairman Kaku. 'I don't think making political donations is absolutely necessary, but as long as it isn't in the form of under-the-table gifts, and is for the good of the country, I'm not totally against them.'

Not only politicians are distrusted by Chairman Kaku. At his behest Canon does not have dealings with the Japanese military either. Though officially non-existent under the American-authored constitution of 1945, the Japanese military is in fact one of the most efficient and best armed in the world. Legally, Japan is only allowed an establishment of ground, air and sea self-defence forces. In reality, however, Japan, with an annual expenditure of around $44.6 billion, ranks third in the world, after Russia ($106.9 billion) and the United States ($278.7 billion), and well above France ($42.7 billion), Germany ($34.8 billion) and the UK ($33.9 billion). There is, then, a vast opportunity for manufacturers to get into the military market, but Canon, while not actually turning down orders, does not actively court military contacts. The non-military posture is long-held and certainly pre-dates the presidency and chairmanship of Kaku, but his experiences of war and survival have strengthened his resolve against the military force and the nationalistic jingoism often spouted by politicians and thriving right-wing groups.

Despite this apparent anti-military stance, Kaku has unusual plans for both the reformation of Japan's military establishment and the education of Japan's younger generation. He explains: 'In my opinion, all countries in the world should live together in peace and cooperation, but this is not as simple as it may sound. In Japan, for instance, many of the younger generation seem to spend all their time demanding their rights without even dreaming that those rights carry responsibilities. And there are a lot of crazy people demanding crazy rights.

'Japanese democracy is not a real democracy, but in order to protect what we have, and prepare for political evolution, we have to start by making people understand their responsibilities to the state and the world. We can do this by introducing a system of public service. I believe that all citizens over eighteen should serve in the defence forces or a Japanese equivalent of the American Peace Corps. Such mandatory programmes would not only give the younger generation a sense of responsibility for Japan's own security, but would also introduce them to Japan's responsibilities as a citizen of the world community.'

Chairman Kaku's survival of Nagasaki has not only made him aware of the dangers of military power without democratic responsibility, but has also made him think very deeply about pollution and the supply and usage of energy. Japan has no significant natural resources for energy production, with only tiny deposits of Japanese oil and gas being found, and Japanese coal being uneconomic to mine. The production of electric energy is therefore predominantly by hydroelectric plants and a large number of nuclear power stations. Japan's climatic and geological environments, characterized by typhoons, a long rainy season and severe earthquakes, make both these forms of energy considerably more dangerous than in other more temperate and stable countries. While hydroelectric power plant disasters can probably be seen as acts of God, nuclear disasters are definitely acts of man, something that Chairman Kaku, having survived once, is understandably opposed to experiencing again.

Even today, after more than fifty years, the memories haven't completely disappeared. With a certain amount of irony, Kaku explains: 'In those days, each morning one of my first acts was to grab hold of a tuft of my hair and pull it. If it didn't come out by the fistful I knew that I would survive another day.' Distrust of nuclear power is more than just a philosophy to this survivor. Under Kaku, Canon has devoted much time and research money to the development of an alternative power source that is safe, non-polluting and economically viable. Solar cell technology is one of Chairman Kaku's pet projects that has also been strongly embraced by company President Fujio Mitarai.

In a new, solar-power R&D centre located between Japan's two ancient capital cities of Kyoto and Nara, development of this clean and non-exhaustible energy source is proceeding apace. Already the project is supplying several domestic premises with electricity at rates competitive with national grid power. What is even better, at least in Chairman Kaku's view, is that unused electricity from solar cells can be sold to the national power companies, thereby reducing both the consumers' bills and the amount of power needed to be generated by nuclear power stations.

There is a long, long way to go, however, before this dream of the chairman is realized. Eiichi Kondo, director and senior general manager of the company's Kyoto research centre, explains. 'If you have a good product and there is an established market, you know that it will sell, as happened with the Bubble Jet Printers we developed. But in solar cell technology there isn't a market yet, and even the technology is experimental and not fully developed. We will have to do everything from developing more efficient solar cells to actually building a market by letting the public know they are available and earning their trust. It is a titanic job, but if, or perhaps I should say when, we succeed we will have helped to solve both the energy shortage and the problem of environmental pollution at the same time. Even if it takes another twenty years, I'm not going to be defeated. The rewards for humanity are just too large to allow such a project to go by the wayside.' No doubt Chairman Kaku would agree. Kondo's attitude is perfectly in line with the chairman's farsighted and humanist views. On the whole, under Kaku's management as president and then chairman, Canon has pursued a business policy of corporate honesty and dignity combined with an unusual level of care for the environment. This rebel definitely has had a cause and pursued it with unrelenting energy throughout his working life.

This cause, though particular to Chairman Kaku, has been distilled from various sources. He especially likes to quote the following: 'Trading should benefit both parties equally by meeting their respective needs . . . When both parties benefit, the advantages are great, but even if a deal is extremely profitable, unless the profit is shared, the benefits will only be small. Profit in this sense refers to, and is inseparable from, morality. It is a truism that where a greedy merchant will demand five, a trader with integrity will only ask for three . . .

'When we compare foreign countries with ours, we notice the linguistic and cultural differences. But when it comes to human nature, there is no difference. It is wrong to concentrate on what distinguishes us from one another while forgetting what we have in common . . . Heaven will not forgive man's deceits. We must not shame our country through selfish actions.

'When you meet a man of virtue in a foreign land, revere him as your father or teacher, learn of his country's customs and follow the ways of that land . . . All men are brothers, and are to be equally loved. When in danger or sickness, or suffering from cold and hunger, you must not hesitate to help each other.'

A hundred and seventy-two years before the American Colonies demonstrated their anger at unfair trade through the Boston Tea Party, and 173 years before the American Declaration of Independence told the world that all men are created equal, the paragraphs quoted above were penned by So-an Suminokura, a major Japanese merchant, in the year 1603.

Born in 1572, the son of a wealthy merchant, Suminokura was already a successful trader at the age of only thirty-one, when in 1603 the shogunate reopened trade links with the outside world through a system called Shuinsen (trade only by ships licensed by the shogunate). So-an, also a respected Confucian scholar, was granted a licence and drafted a set of rules of conduct. Only those who accepted the principle that all men are brothers, and who promised to abide by the rules, were allowed on So-an's ships and thereby out of Japan.

Thus, says Canon Chairman Ryuzaburo Kaku, his philosophy of *kyosei* – living and working together for the common good – is not truly original, even in Japan. He freely admits that he has drawn to a great extent on the thoughts and guidelines of the seventeenth-century trader, Suminokura, and even gives his own personal definition of *kyosei* as simply a modernized version of So-an's concept – 'All people, regardless of race, religion or culture, harmoniously living and working together for many years to come'.

A company, Kaku believes, cannot simply adopt the rules of *kyosei* and become a truly international organization. *Kyosei*, he claims, is the result of a period of corporate evolution which passes through three early stages before culminating in the final stage with a company capable of *kyosei* on a global scale.

The four stages are relatively easily identified. Characteristic of the first is what Kaku calls the 'purely capitalistic corporation' identified in its initial stage of development. As Kaku puts it, 'Though inevitably stimulating the economy, this type of company only benefits the owners and management. Employees are only regarded as means to ends and are generally badly neglected. The result, not unnaturally, leads to labour–management strife and calls for Marxian strategies.'

The second stage of corporate evolution, he continues, is that of 'the company that shares a prosperous future', explaining, 'This type of corporation addresses the shortcomings of the former type, by giving both management and workers a share of the profits and uniting them in a desire to see the company prosper. However, companies in this stage of development are only interested in pursuing greater benefits for company members, and show no interest in the community as a whole. Such an attitude often results in serious pollution problems and environmental disasters.'

At the third stage, says Kaku, if things progress correctly, the evolving organization becomes a 'company assuming local social responsibilities'. Companies in this classification, he continues, 'respect the interests of their own stakeholders – customers, staff, shareholders, suppliers, competitors and the local community. They also try very hard to forward the aims of their individual countries. But, although we can say they accept some social responsibilities, this is only so within their national borders, and in some cases, only within their local boundaries.

'Although this kind of company escapes criticism on a domestic level, it is often the target of considerable censure from other countries in which it operates. This is only natural, because time and time again it is shown to be only interested in domestic matters and to care little or nothing for the international repercussions of its actions. The results of such companies' actions are well known: environmental deterioration, global trade imbalances and developmental inequalities.'

Finally, according to Kaku, a company can enter the fourth stage of evolution, which he describes as 'a corporation assuming global social responsibilities. This kind of company cares for all its direct stakeholders including its local community and beyond. While such a company has excellent labour relations and is a good corporate member of its local community, it also works to fulfil its corporate obligations on a global scale. Its social responsibilities transcend national borders, and it is what can be called a truly global corporation.'

The four stages are thus:

1. A purely capitalistic corporation
2. A company sharing a prosperous future
3. A company assuming local social responsibilities
4. A company assuming global social responsibilities

Chairman Kaku believes that most companies will travel this evolutionary path, but admits that some may get stuck, or choose to remain, in one of the stages prior to achieving the fourth stage of *kyosei*. In general, however, he sees the stages as mainly historical. He believes that Japan, through its unique history, can provide an excellent model for such development.

Up until the fall of the shogunate and the restoration of the Emperor Meiji in 1868, Japan had allowed very little foreign trade and had remained almost totally isolated from contacts with the West. However, once the decision to catch up was made, the country entered an orgy of modernization and development. In the ensuing seventy-seven years, until Japan was atom-bombed into submission in 1945, the nation was a powerhouse of companies in the first stage of development. Huge industrial combines were formed, many of which still exist. Technology was imported and improved. Profits were higher than ever before, and a clique of powerful industrialists held sway over the lives of tens of millions of employees. All individual needs were subsumed by the requirements of the company. Labour organizations were not allowed any strength, and the worker was a mere tool. Working for a company was practically the same as being in the Army – all actions were officially for the good of the Emperor and, therefore, for the good of the state, and there was simply no choice but to follow orders. Any attempt to disobey would be judged as a form of corporate, and possibly national, treason.

With the end of the war, many Japanese corporations were pushed struggling and screaming into the second stage of *kyosei*. Japan under the American-led Occupation was sent off in a diametrically opposed economic direction. The giant industrial combines which had controlled the economy and wielded phenomenal economic and political power were dismantled. Political freedom and universal suffrage were introduced. Labour unions were welcomed, at least in the early days, and companies were encouraged to take on the responsibilities of caring for their work-forces.

During this period, from 1945 until the mid-sixties, Japan experienced phenomenal industrial growth, and each year its citizens became better and better off. There was a downside, however. Companies regarded growth as the be-all and end-all of their existence. Output and profits were all that mattered, and, as a result, the national infrastructure and the natural environment were ignored.

The results of such profit-first policies can be most graphically seen in the harrowing photographs of sufferers of Minamata disease. Throughout the period of post-war rapid growth, little heed was given to the environment and the effect pollution would have on people. In the early 1960s, the first signs of something drastically wrong began to appear in the Kyushu fishing village of Minamata. Cats fed on fish caught in Minamata Bay began to have convulsions, and unfortunately it was not long before people suffered the same fate.

The sickness, known in Japan as *itai-itai* (ouch-ouch) disease, resulted in violent spasms and caused such brittleness in the victims' bones that they could simply snap. It was finally discovered that the condition resulted from the dumping of mercury into Minamata Bay by the Chisso Corporation. Many died and, to this day, many still suffer from the results of this company's lack of social responsibility. In the late 1960s, however, corporate executives at Chisso denied any responsibility and even went to the lengths of hiring gangsters to intimidate victims and stop them from claiming damages. During this period there was no denying the obvious beginnings of the Japanese economic miracle, but it came accompanied by the suffering imposed on many by the uncaring attitudes of companies in stage two of *kyosei* development.

Ultimately, the public outcry against, and the international condemnation of, such disasters forced the Japanese government and corporations to begin to take account of the environment and the people. From the late 1960s until the mid-eighties, many companies can be said to have entered the third stage of *kyosei* and assumed local responsibilities.

During this period, most Japanese corporations began to take a much more public interest in the national community. Strict anti-pollution measures were introduced and life in general became much safer and more comfortable for the average Japanese. Outside Japan, however, the picture was significantly different. Japanese corporations embarked on a rampage through foreign countries. The only interest they had concerning raw materials was price. Rain-forests were destroyed, rivers were polluted, skies blackened and native workers sickened in the corporate drive for cheap materials.

Foreign markets for Japanese goods were only regarded as important if they were profitable. Under MITI (Ministry of International Trade and Industry) leadership, entire Japanese industries cooperated in plans first to infiltrate and then to dominate foreign markets. And it worked. The standard of life in Japan improved rapidly, although Japan's image abroad declined in an almost inverse ratio. Whilst MITI threw every possible barrier in the way of foreign companies trying to operate in Japan, Japanese companies took advantage of American and European free markets to amass the largest trade imbalances the world had ever seen.

For a period in the 1980s, it seemed as if Japan really was set to dominate the developed world. With an almost unbelievable arrogance, Japanese companies and individuals bought the icons of other nations, thereby earning the hatred of many peoples. The Americans, for example, were distraught when a Japanese company bought the Rockefeller Center; the Australians weren't very happy when they heard of a Japanese government proposal to set up retirement centres for ageing Japanese in Queensland, and in the battle for parity the French even went so far as decreeing that all Japanese electronic equipment targeted at France would only be allowed entry via one tiny, previously unheard-of port.

It is not surprising, then, that when the Japanese economic bubble burst in the early 1990s, many foreign powers could not help but appear satisfied with the way things had turned out. When the yen soared to around the ¥80 to the $1 mark, and it looked as though Japan was in real danger of economic implosion, the Japanese did not encounter much international camaraderie. When Japanese investors went broke, and had to sell their golf clubs and office buildings throughout the world, there was unconcealed glee. When Japanese banks failed not only to dominate, but even to register in the global top ten lists, most in the financial world were delighted. And when Japan was finally recognized as just another competitor, not an uncontrollable dominator, the world breathed a collective sigh.

The roller-coaster ride many Japanese companies have experienced during this century has brought many of them, finally, to reassess their roles in the global community. There are now quite a few Japanese corporations that can be judged to be truly international. Both Honda and Sony, for example, are probably more successful and certainly more respected abroad than they are at home. And many others have learnt that long-term stability depends on becoming a good corporate citizen on a multinational stage.

Chairman Kaku admits that, for many companies, the transition from stage three to stage four of *kyosei* will be very difficult, because corporate managers have to learn, first, how to trust and, second, whom to trust. So how does Canon actually go about choosing a *kyosei* partner?

Kaku explains his philosophy. 'When we are thinking of forming a cooperative *kyosei* partnership with a company, we like to really get to know the top management, not just at a purely business level, but on a true friendship basis. We need to know that we can deal with these people on all levels and that they will be truly trustworthy partners.

'Not so long ago we thought we could do a *kyosei* deal with a leading office equipment manufacturer. Unfortunately, we found out that our potential partner organization had rather Machiavellian traits. We decided we couldn't achieve *kyosei* with that company.'

The seemingly perfect *kyosei* partnership for Canon is that achieved with Hewlett-Packard, now the largest marketer of laser-beam printers in the world. Says Takashi Kitamura, now managing director and chief executive of Canon's Peripheral Products Operations, but who once headed the prototype team for the development of laser-beam printers, 'We developed the technology and announced the prototype first, but in 1975 IBM announced that they had also developed a laser printer. At first we were a little disappointed, but then we realized that the IBM approach was to produce a fast, but very big, printer to use with big machines. We, on the other hand, had planned a small-sized, high-speed machine.

'Even so, Canon was still a relatively small company at that time, and when we first developed the technology, there were a lot of doubts as to whether or not we could actually commercialize it successfully. We decided to concentrate on what we were already good at – design, development and manufacturing – and decided to go along the partnership route with marketing and sales-support functions because we didn't know whether we could carry them out on a global scale, and this is where H-P came on the scene.'

Lewis H. Platt, president and CEO of Hewlett-Packard, agrees that his company's relationship with Canon is something beyond the usual. 'We do have a deeper relationship with Canon than with other business partners. It is really seen as a "special" relationship which ends up as a successful relationship for both partners.' He is even optimistic about the future, as a result of the *kyosei* of the past, saying, '[The relationship with Canon] has benefited us tremendously. We were able to acquire high-quality laser print engine technology from them, which allowed us to concentrate our efforts on format and packaging of the product. This helped us make a unique and successful product that is marketed all over the world, now. It has also brought together what each partner knows best. In the foreseeable future, we should see a continuation of the relationship along the lines it is today, but eventually, one partner or the other may want to see some changes, and this would probably be in the form of an extension of the current relationship.' There seems little doubt that Hewlett-Packard is happy with the way things have developed, and there is little doubt that Canon wishes all its *kyosei* partners would be as reliable.

Chairman Kaku continues, 'The deal with the leading office

equipment manufacturer I mentioned earlier was totally different from the agreement we reached with Hewlett-Packard under Mr John Young. With them, and with him in particular, we reached total agreement. We have now been partners for a very long time and I feel that we have reached *kyosei*; in other words, we are truly living and working together for the common good. Both Canon and H-P have benefited from our relationship, but more importantly, we have been able to market laser printers globally on a scale neither one of us could have managed independently, resulting in real prosperity.

'And we expect the partnership to carry on for a long time. Unfortunately, Mr Young is no longer with H-P, but the people who have taken over are following his lead, so we see no reason to believe our trust is in danger. We are happy with the *kyosei* we have achieved with H-P.'

In fact, the visitor to Canon Virginia, in the USA, one of the company's most advanced plants, will see only a single line producing Canon-badged products. Almost the entire output of this huge factory is on behalf of Hewlett-Packard. It may appear strange, at least on the surface, but worldwide sales of laser printers are dominated jointly by Canon and Hewlett-Packard. This is achieved by the fact that Canon, as well as selling its own products, produces engines for many H-P products, thereby making the companies partners. However, where ink-jet printers are concerned, though Canon and H-P developed products independently, they are still both market leaders. Therefore, in this case, the companies are in competition. *Kyosei*, in fact, means that cooperation and competition can be seen as merely different sides of the same coin.

Though probably the most successful of Canon's forays into *kyosei*, Hewlett-Packard is certainly not the only one. Throughout the world, Canon is setting up *kyosei* partnerships with manufacturers, R&D specialists, universities and many other types of organization in the hope, says Kaku, 'that our business will grow naturally, through strategic partnerships, rather than just through a process of acquisition, with the big fish eating the smaller fry'.

Under Ryuzaburo Kaku, first as president, then as chairman, Canon can now claim to have moved from stage three to stage four of *kyosei* development. And Kaku now sees his responsibilities as putting *kyosei* on a national and then international footing. 'When I first came up with the concept of *kyosei*,' he explains, 'it was merely in response to a need to manage Canon more effectively. But now I can see its applications to many other corporations and nations and, in fact, to the world as a whole.

'This pattern of thinking started when I began to wonder how I could express the word *kyosei* in English,' he continues. 'Recently at a meeting of MRA [Moral Re-Armament, a worldwide, non-governmental organization], with the help of several wise Americans and Europeans, I tried to come up with a satisfactory translation, and the consensus was that "living and working together for the common good" was about as internationally acceptable as we could get. Even so, I'm still not quite satisfied. What after all, is "the common good"?

'China, for example, has 1.2 billion people, so their common good could be simply to put enough food into everyone's bellies. This, naturally, differs, say, from the common good of the Israelis, or of the Arabs who feel that their common good depends on the existence, or not, of Israel. This is true of many other areas of the world where there are conflicts. How, for example, can we say that the Protestants and Catholics in Northern Ireland have the same common good? We can't, of course.

'Religions are good, but different, and nations differ very much in histories and cultures, so what is good for one is not necessarily good for another. But, perhaps, the actual concept of partnership that forms the basis of *kyosei* could itself become the global common good of the twenty-first century.

'Often, in the West, the common good is translated as freedom, or sometimes as equality, fraternity or even democracy. This, of course, derives from the common hunter–gatherer history, where people moved on from place to place as necessary. But in Asia, where rice cultivation tied people to one place, there is no nostalgic yearning for the common good of freedom.'

Although he claims not to have any political ambitions himself, Chairman Kaku clearly does have hopes for an extension of *kyosei* to the national and international scenes. He explains: 'I've been working on corporate concepts for over twenty years, and I suppose I have now graduated to attempting to work out a national concept for the Japan of the future.

'Since the Tokugawa Period of around 240 years of isolation ended with the Meiji Restoration in 1868, Japan has spent most of the time, and almost all its energies, on attempts – mostly successful, I admit – to catch up with the developed nations. But now we have to face the fact that the period of catching up is over. Unfortunately, Japan seems only able to understand what has already happened, and appears to lack any vision of what the future should be like. Perhaps more important is the fact that the country just can't seem to decide what Japan's future role on the global stage should be.

'In 1968, exactly 100 years after the Meiji Restoration, Japan's GNP was second in the world, beaten only by the USA. Japan had caught up, but nobody in Japan seemed to realize this. We were a rich nation but we still felt poor. This is probably because if you feel rich, and in fact are rich, you will be expected to lead, and Japan was not ready to lead the world. From this perspective I now feel that Japan's national principle should, like Canon's, be changed to seeking *kyosei* with all humankind instead of blindly pursuing the outdated policy of making Japan rich.

'Specifically speaking, this means changing the catch-up policy followed since Meiji times in at least four ways. Until now, the public sector has taken the lead under the guidance of the government, with the private sector merely hanging on to its coat-tails. This system is known as developmental capitalism, and is considered to be the most efficient form to be followed by a developing country. In Japan, alas, although we can no longer be considered a developing nation, the public sector is still taking the initiative. My first proposal is that the approach should be changed to allow the private sector to take the lead.

'The second change that is needed is for the country to move to a citizens-and-consumers-first orientation and away from the current industry-first approach. This may have been very successful in allowing us to catch up with the West, but is rather like allowing the tail to wag the dog these days.

'The third necessary change is for a shift away from centralization. In the past it was considered most effective to exercise central control, but I now believe that many of the national government's powers should be transferred to local authorities, under what I would call a system of centrally controlled decentralization.

'The fourth change we need is a revolution in education. During the catch-up period a great deal of emphasis was placed, not altogether illogically, on emulating others, or on what is best called fact-concentrated education. Students hardly ever learned why something happened, they were only told how it occurred. From now on, however, we need to emphasize creativity, culture, morality and ethics.

'Only when Japan has done these things can it begin to apply *kyosei* on a global scale to the three major worldwide imbalances: Trade, Income and Generation. *Kyosei* would introduce a partnership of global companies that could eventually do away with international trade imbalances. Such a move would also be able to counter current north—south imbalances in earnings and spending power. Finally, if there was true *kyosei*, conflict between generations could be done away with, and each generation could live healthily and with dignity.'

Despite his dreams of achieving *kyosei* on a global scale, Kaku has currently to satisfy himself with the steps Canon is taking towards achieving the fulfilment of his philosophy. Although the company is making progress, there is still a long way to go. Canon is now represented in almost all parts of the world, but it would be untrue to say that all parts of the world are benefiting equally from relationships with Canon.

In the early days of rapid growth, both in the Japanese economy in general and at Canon in particular, and while the company was in stage two of Kaku's *kyosei* development, the United States and Europe were the obvious marketing targets. Even today, after more than thirty years, and despite a rapidly growing presence in Asia, the United States and Europe are still Canon's most important non-domestic markets. Each accounts for approximately a third of the overall business.

The first foreign market was, of course, America, where a branch office was opened in October 1955. This was followed, in September 1957, by the inauguration of Canon Europa in Geneva, Switzerland. It is safe to say that neither project was an instant success. Despite the relatively high quality of Canon's products at the time, the overall image of Japanese manufacturers worked to make American and European consumers wary of putting their trust in the oriental newcomer. President de Gaulle of France, in a typically undiplomatic way, expressed what many Westerners felt about Japanese industry at the time. When asked if he would be interested in meeting the Japanese prime minister, he replied that he had many more important things to do than 'meet a transistor salesman'. However, Canon persevered, and both markets are now extremely profitable and vital to the company's global plans.

In the United States Canon now has manufacturing subsidiaries in Costa Mesa, California, Newport News, Virginia (3), and Tappahannock, Virginia; as well as North American marketing subsidiaries and affiliates in Burlington, New Jersey (2), Costa Mesa, California, Gardena, California, Irvine, California, Lake Success, New York, Miami, Florida, New York City, Schaumberg, Illinois, Markham, Ontario, and Mississauga, Ontario. In Europe, there are manufacturing subsidiaries in France, Germany, Italy and Scotland, as well as marketing subsidiaries or affiliates in Austria (2), Belgium, the Czech Republic, England (6), Finland, France (2), Germany (3), Holland (2), Hungary, Ireland, Italy (2), Norway, Poland, Scotland, Spain, Sweden and Switzerland (2). There are also American R&D facilities in Costa Mesa, California, and Palo Alto, California, and European facilities in Guildford (2) in the UK and in Cesson-Seveigne, France.

There are, of course, many other marketing subsidiaries and affiliates, R&D centres and manufacturing plants throughout the rest of the world, predominantly in Asia and South America, but the three relatively independent areas of Japan, North America and Europe contribute most to the company's production and sales.

Sales for 1996 also reflected these main areas of Canon's efforts. Japan accounted for 32.4 per cent of sales, North America (USA, Canada and Mexico) for 32.0 per cent and Europe for 27.5 per cent, with the rest of the world only managing a total of 8.1 per cent. In the same year, Canon had 37,431 employees in Japan, 12,170 in Europe, 9,441 in North America, and 16,586 throughout the rest of the world.

It is quite plain to see, therefore, that Canon has a long way to go to become equal partners in *kyosei* with, for example, the Saudis, the Singaporeans or the South Africans. But plans are afoot to change all this, as we shall see in Chapter Nine, with the Asia 15 Project, and new initiatives in Central and South

America. Chairman Kaku believes that it would be wrong for Canon to rush in to Asia or Africa and just use them as bases for cheap production. First, he points out, Canon has never been a manufacturer that relied only on price to sell. 'We are makers of quality,' he says, 'and that will not change. We already have several manufacturing plants throughout Asia. And what it is very important to remember is that they are genuine manufacturing facilities, using the same technologies that we use here in Japan. They are not just assembly plants. Only in this way, by providing real jobs with real technologies, will we be able to raise the standards of living throughout Asia to the levels where we will automatically produce markets for our own goods.'

Outside Asia, however, Kaku admits that Canon is not really advancing very far. 'It is easy to forget Africa and the Middle East. They are both far from Japan and don't figure in our thoughts as much as Europe, Asia and America. But to do so would be stupid and arrogant.

'Unfortunately, as a business it is difficult to justify investing great amounts in these areas. There just isn't a large enough market yet. What we must first do is upgrade their economies and social structure. Once we have improved social, economic and industrial structures in these areas, we can start getting involved in *kyosei* partnerships.'

It is very doubtful that Chairman Kaku will remain at Canon long enough to see more than the seeds of these dreams sown. It will be up to the next generation of leaders to take up the baton. And in this respect Canon is extremely lucky to have the internationalist Fujio Mitarai in the president's chair. Mitarai plans a step-by-step approach to building markets in developing countries.

The first target, he says, is Asia. 'We are currently building up sales in the developing economies of Asia, particularly China. They may not be particularly wealthy right now, but there is a very good chance they will be in the coming century. If Asia remains peaceful, which I think it will, consumption is likely to expand rapidly at such a pace that it will soon outstrip the United States. And I really think this is going to happen much more quickly than many people expect.'

Mitarai, though sounding very optimistic about sales, does not expect an easy life in Asia. 'Our aim in Asia, as in the rest of the world, is decentralization. We ultimately want to have an independent unit operating in each country. That is the aim. But it is not achievable in the short term, because we don't have the people, and getting them could take years.

'The people we need to employ will have to learn about and understand the Canon way of doing business. The Japanese at Canon will be involved, of course, because we are still a Japan-based company. But this doesn't mean to say I want Japanese running Canon's Asian subsidiaries. We will be looking for managers of any nationality as long as they understand Canon's philosophy and are multicultural.'

Canon has already started to select Japanese employees who have shown interest in becoming Asian specialists, but, says Mitarai, 'Frankly speaking, it is not easy to find many people willing to go to poorer countries on what could, I suppose, be called hardship postings. On the other hand, younger people are changing, as are many of the developing countries throughout Asia, and I think there will be a reasonable number of young people who really want to live and work in Asia. What is important, however, is that we choose the right ones.

'At Canon we don't force anyone to go abroad. We try to choose the person we think will be most effective in a certain job in a certain country and then persuade them to go, but there is no coercion.

'To deal with the coming Asian century, we have recently started an Asia Trainee Programme. The people on this have all responded to questionnaires asking if they would like to be stationed in Asia. Before they can even be considered for a specific job in a given country, they are first sent for a year to a local university where they learn the language and study the culture. Then the following year is spent as a trainee in a Canon operation in the same country. Only then would they be assigned as a genuine member of Canon's staff in that country.'

As well as emphasizing careful selection of the people it hires or sends to new markets and new manufacturing plants, Canon believes it has a responsibility to treat each person and each country with equal dignity and care. Just because, for example, emission controls are stricter in California than in China, it does not mean, Canon believes, that a Chinese factory should produce more pollution than a Californian plant. The company is extremely proud of its record in this area, and applies not only the strictest local environmental regulations, but the most stringent global levels to all its factories worldwide. Thus, if the American regulations on chlorofluorocarbons (CFCs) are the most severe, Canon will not only abide by, or better them, in the United States, but will also enforce the same rules at every other plant anywhere in the world.

There are specific environmental areas in which Canon believes it is leading the world. For example, the company conducts environmental impact examinations for every product during the design stage. It assesses how a product's environmental impact can be reduced at each stage of its life, beginning with R&D through manufacture, distribution, customer usage and eventual disposal. After such an assessment, Canon makes the necessary adjustments to the projected product and only then can production begin.

This policy has already yielded considerable benefits. By the end of 1992, for example, the company had completely eliminated the use of CFCs used in lens cleaning, and by the end of 1993 had discontinued the use of trichloroethane for the cleaning of metal parts. These goals were achieved both through finding unharmful substitutes and by changing component materials.

Since 1992, in an attempt to cut down on the use of plastics as well as halt the depletion of the rain-forests, Canon has been using recycled-paper-pulp moulds as buffer material in place of polystyrene in packaging. The company has also switched from wooden to cardboard pallets and fibreboard slip sheets for transporting large office machines. All these materials can of course be recycled after use.

As the world's largest lens manufacturer, Canon has also been conducting wide-ranging experiments and cooperating with optical glass manufacturers on the development of lead-free glass. The research, which commenced in 1991, has already produced some forty types of lens free from harmful lead.

Since July 1992 Canon has been using plastic material identifiers which conform to ISO standards, and has been sorting and recycling plastics by type. Initially the company used identifiers on moulded-plastic photocopier parts weighing more than 100 grams (3½ ounces), but in 1993 reduced the part weight to 50 grams, which resulted in a massive increase in the company's plastic recycling ratio.

All these examples, however, pale by comparison with what the company is doing in Scotland, Virginia and China. In 1992 Canon began the re-manufacturing of copying machines at its Virginia factory, and in 1993 opened a factory dedicated to copying-machine re-manufacture in Scotland. The impact on the environment is obviously less serious if a part if re-used in its existing form, rather than being converted back into its raw materials before re-use. In Virginia and Scotland, therefore, outmoded copying machines are disassembled and the parts rigorously tested, strictly graded, and when possible used again in new machines. Before the machines are shipped, they are tested to ensure they meet all the standards of machines made from totally new parts.

The life of a copying machine, however, is still considerably longer than that of a toner cartridge, and with millions being used throughout the world, Canon decided to do something about that too. In 1990 the company launched a worldwide recycling programme for toner cartridges used in LBPs' laser facsimile machines and personal copiers. The cartridges are collected in various centres throughout the world before being shipped to the company's Dalian, China, plant for disassembly.

Selected components are reduced to their raw materials for recycling, and others, after strict testing, are re-used in new cartridges. The aim of this project has been to reduce considerably the amount of virgin materials used in new cartridge production and, by so doing, significantly lower the associated carbon emissions. By the end of 1996, the company had already collected and recycled more than 20 million units.

As the company continues to expand throughout the globe, President Mitarai claims there will be even more ecology-minded steps taking place, and no Canon plant in any country will operate under any but the strictest environmental controls. And, says Chairman Kaku, 'Canon will continue to evolve into a company that will lead the world in the evolution of *kyosei*, living and working together for the common good.'

Perhaps the final word should come from an independent observer, journalist Toru Arai: 'Canon may not be a revolutionary company, but it does thoughtfully care for the needs of its employees and society in general.'

CHAPTER FIVE

For some years after the end of the war, the few Japanese lucky enough to travel outside the country, and many non-Japanese, particularly members of the Occupation forces, made quite a profitable sideline selling their duty-free Johnnie Walker Red Label whisky to the alcohol-loving, luxury-starved Japanese. During the early months of 1974, however, Japanese returning from overseas trips, and foreigners visiting Japan, were asked by friends in the country to bring them another item from abroad, something special that just couldn't be found in Japan – toilet rolls.

The 1973 oil crisis had different effects on different nations. Throughout Europe, the queues at petrol stations were often up to a mile long, and the British government even went so far as preparing rationing coupons, though these were never actually issued. Japan, however, took a more pragmatic approach to petrol. The prices were simply raised to match supply and demand, with the result that those who had the money and really wanted to buy fuel could do so without having to queue, while others, particularly the less well-off, simply went without. This pragmatic approach wasn't carried over to other products, however. For some reason a rumour swept the country that the oil crisis was somehow affecting the production of toilet tissue, and the race was on. Housewives were seen laden down with scores of rolls, businessmen were caught creeping out of restaurant and hotel rest-rooms with stolen tissues under their jackets, and shops sold out within minutes of getting new stocks. As has been remarked many times by many people, Japan certainly is different.

Between these two periods of shortages – the first genuine

and the second imaginary – Japan had experienced almost three decades of superlative economic growth and rapid increase in the standard of living. The country had evolved from a defeated fascist state into Asia's leading parliamentary democracy. Tokyo had hosted the Olympic Games, the first ever held in Asia, and the world was in awe of the Shinkansen (Bullet Train), the fastest means of land transport on the planet. New highways had been built, new subway lines constructed, the mini-skirt, the maxi-skirt and flares had all been experienced, and the Beatles had played Tokyo. Japan had never before experienced such a sustained period of economic growth and burgeoning prosperity.

And at Canon things were no different from anywhere else in the country. With the opening in 1951 of the company's new headquarters and plant in Shimomaruko on the outskirts of Tokyo, and the worldwide distribution agreement with Hong Kong-based trading house Jardine Matheson concluded in the same year, Canon looked set for the success in which founder Takeshi Mitarai had always believed. No longer was production bedevilled by outdated production facilities. The new factory was one of the finest and most modern anywhere in Japan. The morale-boosting move to the recently opened premises was also the signal for the first and probably the greatest period of innovation and growth the company has ever known.

Though recognized predominantly as a maker of cameras, Canon had already by the early 1940s diversified into medical equipment and various other optical technology applications, including the manufacture of a comprehensive range of camera lenses employing the latest, post-war optical theories. Between 1946 and 1953 the company's first truly versatile collection of lenses was launched, ranging from wide-angle to telephoto. This range not only provided the company with another successful consumer line, but can also be said to have formed the basis of Canon's best-selling lenses lines of today.

And it wasn't just in product categories that the company was beginning to flex its muscles. In 1955 Canon began its first very tentative steps towards globalization with the opening of its first overseas branch in New York. This was followed two years later, in 1957, by the establishment of Canon Europa, sole distributor for Europe. The early dreams of Canon could still be seen in the choice of Geneva as the home of the company's European headquarters. Instead of opting for the thriving, mass-production economies of, say, France or one of the Benelux countries, Canon based itself in the land-locked, mountainous, high-tech, high-quality, no-exchange-control but low-volume atmosphere of Switzerland. Eleven years later, however, idealism was to be dropped and reality would set in when the company relocated Canon Europa to a much more sensible distribution centre in Amsterdam.

Aside from such first international steps, the fifties were really the decade of innovative products. Between 1956 and 1958 four new camera models were introduced, as well as an even further-expanded range of lenses. For the first time in Japanese history, the young generation of the 1950s discovered leisure and leisure activities, and loved to record these by means of photography, thereby fuelling Japan's camera boom and Canon's profits. But some of the new sophisticates wanted even more, and so in 1956 Canon met their requirements with another technological breakthrough, the launch of the company's first cine-camera, the Canon 8T. It was so successful that in one fell swoop Canon became Japan's leading cine-camera manufacturer.

Throughout the rest of the decade there was no respite from technological advancement. New product followed new product, with the 1959 launch of the Model P camera representing Canon's last major successful innovation of the fifties. Prior to the design and commercialization of the Model P, it had only been possible to produce top-quality cameras in small production runs because of the labour-intensive system of manufacturing then employed. However, beginning with the manufacture of the Model P, Canon streamlined the production process and introduced a conveyor-belt production-line system. This, combined with a much more strict selection of raw materials and the standardization of mechanical parts, ensured the company of considerably higher-quality levels than had ever been possible before. A new era of mass-produced, reliable and lower-priced cameras had begun.

In May of the same year, 1959, after several years of intense research and development, Canon achieved a further technical breakthrough with the launch of the Canoflex, a single-lens reflex (SLR) camera, the first of a long line of SLR successes. This was followed a mere two years later, in 1961, by the development of the world's first mass-produced lens-shutter-type electric eye camera, the Canonet. The new mass-production techniques now employed at Shimomaruko and the company's other plants had enabled them to turn out larger quantities of higher-quality cameras at lower prices than ever before, further fuelling Japan's photography boom. And even into the sixties the speed of development didn't slow down. Throughout that decade Canon continued to innovate and expand. By 1963 the development of the first autofocus camera was announced, and in 1964 the FX, featuring a radical improvement in SLR technology, was launched.

Although cameras and lenses were Canon's bread and butter, by the end of the fifties the company was already looking for a larger slice of the consumer pie. Its first attempt at capturing a completely new market came with the launch of the Synchroreader in 1959. This was a revolutionary new device that combined book and recording machine, and was based on the original concept of Professor Yasushi Hoshino, a brilliant faculty member of the Tokyo Institute of Technology.

The operating principles of the Synchroreader were

completely new. Three magnetic heads, located concentrically on a turntable, were sequentially put in contact with the magnetized underside of a sheet of a set width. The turntable was made to move along the length of the sheet with the result that the magnetized heads were able both to record sounds and replay them on demand. In this function, it was not that different from a tape-recorder, but the Synchroreader was unique in another way. By looking at the top of the magnetized sheet while the machine was reproducing the recorded words, the user was able to read the script at the same time. The fact that the actions of sound reproduction and reading were synchronized gave rise to the product name.

Canon was able to market the Synchroreader only two years after deciding to go ahead with the project, a remarkably rapid development pace. This had only been made possible by the company's massive investment in technology and production machinery, and year-long recruitment campaigns to find the best researchers and designers in Japan. In fact, it would probably be safe to say that the spirit of the Synchroreader was the progenitor of Canon's R&D style of today. The camera manufacturer was beginning to spread its wings.

The designers, of course, and even some sections of the media, were excited by the potential for such an appliance, particularly, say, in language education. Through the use of the Synchroreader, students of languages would be able to read and listen to the correct pronunciation at the same time. In fact, the Synchroreader attracted so much attention that, according to the *Asahi Journal* of 15 March 1959, 'Even before the product [the Synchroreader] has been put on the market, it has caused more of a fuss than salcomycin and the ¥10,000 note.' This was praise indeed, since salcomycin was considered to be a new antibiotic wonder drug, and the ¥10,000 note ($27.8) was, and still is, the largest ever put into circulation in Japan.

Unfortunately, advance sales estimates turned out to have been extremely over-optimistic. When the Synchroreader went on sale it was not well received; and only 850 models were sold in the first six months. There are several reasons for its failure, including the price of ¥135,000 ($375.30), ridiculously high at the time, and the fact that other manufacturers were launching similar products at the same time, and at considerably lower prices.

Even the Synchroreader's unique selling point of combining recording and playback functions with that of a book didn't impress consumers. As it turned out, most people, even the targeted language students, preferred to buy books and audiotapes or records separately. The Synchroreader was doomed before it really began.

Canon wasn't ready to give up, however. In January 1960 the company launched a stripped-down, lower-specification and cheaper version of the Synchroreader, the Sheet Recorder. This model had only one magnetic head, which was made to move in a spiral fashion, unlike the Synchroreader's more sophisticated three-head system. Instead of going it alone again, Canon had developed the Sheet Recorder in conjunction with Tokyo Shibaura Electric Inc., the predecessor of today's Toshiba Corp. Canon manufactured the product and Tokyo Shibaura was in charge of sales. Even so, the Sheet Recorder was no more successful than the Synchroreader, and was withdrawn from the market as a failure. These two products represented Canon's first major diversification into completely new product lines far removed from the company's core technologies, and, though both were failures, they did have the effect of invigorating Canon's desire for technological innovation.

There were many reasons for the failure of the Synchroreader and the Sheet Recorder, including a lack of sufficient technical ability, ineffective market research and poor marketing. But the true reason was one that was to plague Canon for many years and, some say, is still a serious problem for the company. The engineers and designers simply didn't bother to find out if anyone wanted to buy the product. They knew they had designed a superb appliance that worked excellently, but nobody seemed to have asked whether or not the public would be willing to pay several months' average salary for a machine that made noises while the user read words. As it turned out, almost nobody was prepared to do so.

This was the beginning of a period during which Canon was to become a design-led company. There were several other failures before a more rational approach to market research and marketing was adopted, and some commentators and even customers believe Canon still hasn't learnt its lesson. Hiroshi Yoshihara, vice-president of Equity Research at Salomon Brothers Asia Limited in Tokyo, says, 'A possible problem for Canon is their inability to understand what the consumer wants. Of course engineers must believe their products are the best, but sometimes the consumer is only interested in price and not the absolute latest technology. Because Canon is engineer-led there is a possibility of completely misjudging the market and launching products that simply aren't wanted.'

A major Canon customer, Keisuke Fujita, general manager of Camera-no-Kimura, a major chain retailer, also worries about the company's marketing skills, even today. 'In general I'm very happy with the popular and attractive products Canon provide, but they need to drastically improve their dealer information packages. They are nearly always late, and just don't give us enough time to prepare ourselves for new products. In the old days, makers only used to change camera models every ten years or so, but now the turnaround is down to a year or less, and the marketing people simply haven't adjusted.'

The problems may still exist, but in the early 1960s they were surfacing for the first time. In a typically Japanese act of contrition and assumption of personal responsibility over the Synchroreader, Canon founder Takeshi Mitarai shouldered the blame, saying, 'What happened was all due to my carelessness. It isn't anyone else's fault. We must deal with this situation as well as we can and try to make something positive out of our misfortune.'

As it turned out, the Synchroreader débâcle was not as bad as it seemed at first, and probably, strangely enough, helped Canon in the long run. After the product had been withdrawn from the market, Canon was left with a new 250,000-square-metre (290,000-square-yard) plant which it had purchased in September 1958 from Mitsui Chemical Industries Inc. specifically for Synchroreader production. The company had also been allowed to import quite a large amount of production machinery and equipment, again specifically for Synchroreader production. At the time, the import of production machinery and equipment was under the iron control of the Ministry of International Trade and Industry (MITI), which had very set ways and concrete ideas on which industries it would support and nurture. A company would never have been allowed to import the plant if it had been intended for camera manufacture, because MITI considered the camera business to be already crowded and over-competitive. But the Ministry, after being shown plans of the Synchroreader, had been impressed with the potential of the new product, and had granted Canon the licences to import the machinery. This, of course, meant that even after the project had been dropped, Canon had a vast amount of the latest production equipment standing idle.

Although the Synchroreader had failed, it was still evident that Canon's continued growth depended on diversification. Accordingly, the first five-year plan to branch out into the office equipment field was adopted in 1962. By 1964, the year of the Tokyo Olympics, Canon had begun an aggressive move to diversify with the introduction of an electronic calculator line. Today it is difficult to believe that only just over thirty years ago the abacus and the slide-rule were about the nearest society had to a calculating machine. Canon recognized the potential demand and set its researchers on to the problem of developing a fully electronic calculator.

The researchers again fulfilled all the demands of management, and in 1964 the world's first ten-key desk-top electronic calcu-lator, the Canola 130, was introduced and met with great initial success. Here again, however, Canon followed the engineer-led path, and within a few short years, competitors had stripped the market away from them. While Canon was stressing the high specifications and superlative quality of production of its machines, other specialist companies like Casio and Sharp were out marketing much cheaper calculators, through well-organized retail systems. This didn't dampen Canon's desire for technical innovation and diversification, however, and calculators were followed by the company's entry into the coated paper copier market, with the development in 1965 of an electrofax copier model, the Canofax 1000. This in turn was capped in 1968 with entry into the plain paper copier (PPC) market with the revolutionary Canon NP.

This move away from camera manufacturing was one of lasting significance to Canon's fortunes. Prior to this time, unlike those camera manufacturers selling film and other consumables, Canon's added value ended with the sale of a camera. A product line that offered a steady source of income from the sale of consumables was considered an essential requirement for growth. The copier, which generated income from paper and toner as well as the machine itself, was seen at the perfect choice. There was only one major obstacle: Xerox seemed to have a stranglehold on the plain paper copier market with over 600 patents. Even so, the decision was taken to start research and come up with

Canon's own unique technology in the area. Most competitors thought that Canon had finally bitten off more than it could chew, but once again the company's brilliant engineers proved the doubters wrong.

A small task-force of engineers spearheaded Canon's research into electrostatic copying. The fact that the members of the group, including Dr Keizo Yamaji, a former vice-chairman and current honorary adviser, and Hiroshi Tanaka, now vice-chairman, are all now prominent in the top echelons of Canon's management, proves how vital the development was.

Canon first entered the market in 1965 with the Canofax 1000, a coated paper copier, followed by the CanAll series which used the electrofax copying process. The company has never looked back, and the photocopier market is now one of the keys to Canon's global success.

Following these forays into diversification, Canon's product lines were built on the triple foundation of precision optics, precision engineering and electronics. Precision optics and precision engineering were the specialities on which Canon's reputation had been built during its first three decades. Electronics, however, a new field of development that began with the Synchroreader and the electronic calculators, was gradually introduced across the whole range of Canon's product lines: cameras, medical equipment, industrial optical equipment, microfilm systems copiers and other systems equipment. In addition, wholly new product lines were developed in communications and business machines. Synergy was the principal aim. Production in 1976 of the Canon AE-1 camera was its first achievement. The AE-1 featured shutter priority aperture control and other completely automated mechanisms controlled by a built-in microprocessor. In the copier field, relay and microswitch mechanisms of solid state electronics design achieved a reduction in production costs and increased reliability. Microfilm and computer technologies were combined to make computer-output microfilm equipment. Precision optical engineering technology gave rise to the non-mydriatic retinal camera. Recording, laser and electrophotographic technologies were combined in computerized printing systems. Yet despite this effort to achieve a synergy of related technologies, in the first half of 1975 Canon suffered its first major reversal since the war, when the payment of a dividend was suspended.

Part of the problem was circumstantial. Demand for existing products declined as a result of the recession following the first oil crisis. Canon's hasty entry into the low-priced calculator market, without first having established suitable distribution channels, posed still another set of difficulties. But the problems ran deeper than that. Simply put, Canon was experiencing a managerial crisis. Top management lacked coherence and direction; the company's inflexible corporate structure made it impossible to deal effectively with diversification, and insufficient attention had been paid to the rationalization of production. In a sense, Canon had grown too much, too fast. Or, as Ryuzaburo Kaku, the present chairman, put it, 'Canon was like a ship that constantly changes course and ends up nowhere.'

The oil crisis that struck Japan and the rest of the Western industralized world also exerted a considerable influence on Canon's operations. Canon Inc.'s sales had continued to grow smoothly after passing the ¥50 billion ($188 million) mark in 1972, but entering the second half of 1974 sales began to slow. Slowing profit growth had initially occurred in the first half of 1974, when profits stood at ¥2.1 billion ($72 million), the same as in the second half of 1973. The main reasons for the slump in profits were abnormal price increases due to the oil crisis, increases in the costs of materials, subcontracting and personnel, and inefficient use of capital owing to excess inventory.

Moreover, a problem of quality that arose in the Panther series of electronic calculators, which were put on the market in the spring of 1974, meant that they didn't sell. The result was an unexpected increase in inventory, mostly of electronic calculators. This put tremendous pressure on Canon's operations. In the first half of 1975, the company went into the red for the first time since its stocks had been listed. Accounting reports from that period describe the situation as follows: 'The influence of the recession is the basic cause of the worsening in performance, but more specifically in Canon's case, the slump in the sales of electronic calculators has become the greatest factor. Since last year, demand has been growing for personal calculators in the electronic calculator market but Canon has been unable to advance by seizing this opportunity. Also there have been problems with the cost and the technical aspects of our products, so that we were smothered in excess inventory of electronic calculators and the like in the beginning of the current period. Because we have tried in this period to clear the inventory, profits have experienced a large drop and performance has been forced even lower than it was in the previous period. To summarize the figures, sales in this period have come to ¥33,784.5 million [$112 million], 6 per cent lower than in the previous period. In terms of profit and loss, there has been a loss of ¥171.7 million [$5.7 million].'

This crisis led relentlessly to the secret emergency meetings, the adoption of Ryuzaburo Kaku's Premier Company Plan, his eventual promotion to president and then chairman, the adoption of the *kyosei* philosophy, and Canon's eventual globalization. As the old saying goes, 'It's an ill wind that blows no good.'

CHAPTER SIX

When a foreigner arrives in Japan, he or she is often surprised by the remarkable level of conformity. Even the non-conformists conform. Punks have exactly the same hair colour and hairstyle and, even more surprisingly, are extremely polite to old people. Old men who have always worn white shirts and neckties during their working life, all sport Texas style bootlace ties when retired. Artists and girls who work in flower-shops all wear berets. Schoolgirls rebel about school uniforms by wearing baggy socks – but they all wear them, just like a uniform. Hardly any Japanese would dream of crossing a road against a red pedestrian signal, even if they could see that there were no vehicles in sight for over a mile.

The list is endless, and the Japanese penchant for conformity is typified by the proverb stating that the nail that sticks up in a shoe is very quickly knocked down. No, individualism is not considered a good thing in Japan. Even so, equality is not the way of the Japanese, either. Children are treated like miniature gods and goddesses. They can do no wrong, with the result that Japan has many of the noisiest, rudest, greediest and downright spoilt brats in existence.

Old people are treated with a great deal of respect, at least on the surface, even if they are ignored when real opinions are sought. And university students are expected to stay drunk and lazy for the four years it takes them to get degrees. Only in the much-vaunted Japanese work-force does the foreigner expect to find equality. But even here, he will be disappointed. Women can almost always forget their dreams of promotion and career fulfilment. Non-university graduates generally do not even get a look in at the betterment stakes. And the graduates of the supposedly best universities, Tokyo and Kyoto in the public sector, and Keio and Waseda in the private, can expect to get offered jobs at the best companies and hope to get more speedy promotion than other less exalted people.

The directors of Canon claim that their company is different. They say that Canon offers sexual, racial and intellectual equality. But do their employees agree with them? Are people given equal opportunity despite differences in job description, sex or ethnic origin? Canon employees have differing views. Naturally enough, some factory workers feel they don't have equal opportunities on tests with their university-educated fellow employees. And older workers who have already benefited from the system feel more positive about it than younger employees who are just starting the climb up the corporate ladder. And foreigners? Well, it depends how they define equality and how equal they actually want to be.

One female employee, a twenty-two-year veteran of the Ami, Ibaragi prefecture, plant felt basically positive about employment opportunities and the promotion system. 'I'm now forty-one and while most of my contemporaries are married and have left the company, I have decided to make a career at Canon. I've never worked anywhere else, so I can't really make comparisons, but when I talk to friends working elsewhere, it is clear that my salary is better. Also, many of the women I know in other companies weren't given responsibility. In Canon, however, when I had learned how to do the job well, I was given respons-ibility. That's important. I get paid well, but I'm expected to work very hard for it. It's just the same as if I was a man.

'I'm not so sure about the examination system, though. They say it's equal, and it certainly is more equal today than when I joined. In those days, women weren't allowed to take the examination under the same conditions as men. This, of course, meant that many women just lost heart and didn't even bother. It was obvious they weren't being treated as equals. But that has been corrected now and all employees can take the test at the same time.

'Even so, I don't think the system is completely fair. For example, the examination depends very heavily on essay answers, and because during their early years in the company men are given broader job experience and opportunities, they have a distinct advantage in experience over women. But this doesn't change the fact that because of my position I am treated as a *sempai* [master] within the company, and looked on as an equal of men.'

Certain aspects of this woman's worries were mirrored by fellow female factory workers. One, who has worked in the factory's administration department for eleven years, added, 'I don't think examinations for promotion are necessarily good news. Some people are just better at exams than others. But I have to admit that the system works quite well. In some companies I know women aren't even allowed to take the tests, so at least we are better off in that respect.'

Even some of the younger, thus nearer to school age, workers were not completely happy with the system. One, who works in product assembly, was particularly wary of academic tests. 'I don't agree with the test system. There are those who can do a job well but can't express themselves well on paper. They are at a disadvantage. Promotion should be decided by work ability, not examination deftness.'

The men at the Ami plant, however, were much more positive about the promotion system. Masaaki Ogata, who joined Canon in 1977, said, 'It's a fair system. Fifty per cent of your promotion prospects depend on the test and the other fifty are a result of work evaluation. This gives everyone an equal chance.' Some, however, were a little worried about on-the-job evaluation, feeling that it may not be as objective as it should be. Koichi Watanabe, with Canon since 1981, said, 'The system is not bad, but it could be improved. In a few rare cases, because of a lack of a standard evaluation system in departments or countries with different working methods, it could fail the individual. For example, if an employee has been stationed abroad, he or she may not have been evaluated in the same way as someone who had stayed in Japan. This could damage future prospects.' This point was echoed by Kazuyuki Michiyama, who joined Canon in 1991. 'The system is basically fair. The written part is acceptable, but I'm a little wary of how a boss evaluates his workers. I think this can be a little too subjective.'

Office workers at Canon's Shimomaruko headquarters tended to be split mainly by age and, of course, sex. Men in their forties were inclined to favour the status quo, as they'd already gone through the examination mill and were looking forward to reaping the benefits. Men in their thirties, however, still held out hope of change. Takahiro Kubo, who works on colour laser copier development, said, 'I'd change the system, especially concerning salary levels. In a few cases, Canon has been too kind and rewarded some people because of their ability in tests, and not by evaluating them through the results of their work. We should introduce a system that would reward hard work and brilliance. If you accomplish something good for the company you should be able to expect a good reward. Western-style payment, at least in this respect, is better than the more egalitarian Japanese system. But of course to be really fair, both collaboration and competition are necessary.'

Women headquarters employees, irrespective of their age, felt that Canon did not offer equal opportunities but was, so they said, at least moving in the right direction. Ms Naomi Yabe, who joined Canon in 1974, explained: 'When I joined the company I was really shocked at how differently the men and women were trained. It seemed that men had real jobs and women were merely "assistants". Over the years, though, things have got much better. I don't really think it is a sex matter. Giving equality means giving responsibility, and most Japanese companies don't give anyone any individual responsibility – whether male or female.'

Ms Asako Suzuki, at Canon since 1986, was more blunt. 'The year I joined was the same year the government enacted the equal opportunities law. Canon kept talking about it, but didn't seem to know what to do to achieve it. Women still do not have equality, no matter what anyone tells you. Of course some women succeed, but they have to work three to five times harder than men to get promoted. Mind you, I'm not downhearted. In a way I feel a little like a suffragette.'

And the old excuses still continue, no matter what the directors may say. As one woman, after seven years with the company, put it: 'When I joined in 1990, all the male freshmen were given sales training, but the women weren't. We asked why we couldn't take part and were told that sales training would be too hard on women.' Ms Yukiko Sakimoto, who also joined Canon in 1990, was even more straightforward: 'When I joined there were already laws about sexual equality, so I took it for granted. In reality, though, I've never seen a male secretary or filing clerk in Canon.'

On the whole, possibly the most that can be said for Canon is that it is trying more than many other companies to bring about equality, on both an intellectual and a sexual basis. In a land where until this year (1997) there was a law strictly limiting the amount of overtime work a woman could be asked to do, while allowing employers to work their men into the ground, this is a relatively giant step forward.

Equality, however, is not just a question of intelligence or sex.

In many companies, the colour of the employee's skin will still make a difference in the promotion stakes. So how are the non-Japanese regular employees at Canon's Shimomaruko head-quarters treated? Tad M. Yotsuuye, an American of Japanese parentage from Tacoma, Washington, said, 'About five years ago, after studying Japanese in Osaka, I was thinking of returning home to the States, when I heard about possible jobs at either Mitsubishi Electric or Canon. I used to work for the Bank of Tokyo in the US, but had left after realizing that the only way you could get promotion was to be born Japanese. So, although I liked the idea of working for a Japanese company in Japan, I had three stipulations. First, I wanted to be a regular employee and not just on a contract. Second, I wanted to work in corporate headquarters, not as the professional *gaijin* at some branch office. And third, because of my work experience, I wanted to work in finance.

'When I was interviewed, both companies agreed to these conditions, but Mitsubishi later changed its mind and suggested I worked for a subsidiary. So I decided to come to Canon, and since then I've been in the capital markets department, where I help to arrange long-term finance.

'I suppose I'm treated as equally as can be expected, considering my imperfect Japanese language level. Because of this, I don't think they can ever regard me as a complete equal, and I wouldn't expect it. I wouldn't mind being transferred to another place in Japan, but here again, language would be a barrier. At the moment, most of my business on the markets is in English, and when the Japanese staff talk to me in Japanese they take care to use language I can understand. I suppose what I'd really like is to get assigned back to the States.'

Yotsuuye obviously likes Japan and Canon, but does not consider himself to be a typical Japanese employee. The company's paternalistic culture also irritates him. 'I'd like the company to stop acting like my parents. They seem to be watching over me all the time. I know it is the Japanese way, but I am an American, after all, and I'm a big boy. For example, when I was living in a dormitory, an old woman who lived near by complained to the company that she'd seen women enter at night and not leave until morning. Now, this is in a dormitory where all the boarders are adult, university-educated businessmen. In America, she'd have been told to mind her own business, but here in Japan, the company told us to stop inviting women.

'Anyway, a dorm meeting was called. There really was no point, because a rule is a rule in Japan and it won't be changed just because it's outdated or just plain silly. The outcome was as I'd expected: lots of people spoke and, eventually, all agreed to do nothing that would upset our pseudo-parents.

'On the whole, though, the people at Canon have been great. I don't think equality is simply a matter of corporate culture. It depends a lot on society, and Japanese society definitely doesn't treat the foreigner as an equal. Japanese never expect a Caucasian or an African to speak Japanese. When they look at me, however, they see a Japanese, and when I speak imperfectly they treat me more as a retarded Japanese rather than an American who's studying the language. This kind of equality I can do without.'

Yotsuuye, it seems, will be more than willing to return to America. After a reasonably long time in Japan he still feels the outsider, but as he says, he is an outsider to society, not to Canon.

Lew Kim Wei is Malaysian, and graduated from university in Tokyo before joining Canon. He is fluent in Japanese and says he chose Japan because he could use his knowledge of Chinese characters and wouldn't have to speak English. He wants to stay permanently in Japan, although he admits he'd like to retire somewhere near the sea, and warm – 'Perhaps Hawaii?'

Regarding equality, he said, 'In Canon I now feel very free. During the first two years I was controlled very much by my bosses, but since last year I've had the freedom to propose ideas and get the help of my supervisor. Now he treats me just the same as any Japanese worker.

'Yes, I think I'm treated equally, but if I wasn't able to speak Japanese I don't think I would be. And that's fair enough. Even now, though, if my colleagues are explaining something in Japanese they take care to make sure I understand and to use vocabulary that I can get.

'As a permanent employee, I would of course be willing to go wherever the company chose to send me. However, as my speciality is in cameras it is most likely that I would be sent to Taiwan, where we manufacture them. I'd welcome the experience, but I'd want to return to Japan after two or three years.

'The negative aspects of my life are not to do with Canon. I miss my family, don't like raw fish, and find it awfully cold over here. But I can survive. The people at Canon are excellent, but in Japanese society as a whole I find the people rather cold. They don't seem as if they want to have any contact with other Asians, and don't even speak to us when we go shopping.'

Despite some obvious problems of integration into Japanese society, not Canon, Lew Kim Wei feels treated an as equal, and sees his working life as a member of the Canon family. There are, however, some non-Japanese who are chosen for their specific skills and who simply get on with the job without caring whether or not their Japanese counterparts regard them as equals. Dr Aruna Rohra is such a Canon employee. An Indian, she has a doctorate in physics from Delhi, and lectured at universities in South America and at Trinity College, Dublin, before joining Canon twelve years ago.

Dr Rohra explained: 'How I came to get this job is interesting. You meet the same people at conferences all over the world. One of the people I'd got to know well was from Canon. When I met him again at a conference somewhere he asked me what

I was doing. I told him I was looking for a job, and asked him if he'd got one for me. A few weeks later Dr Hajime Mitarai, who had been on a business trip to England, flew over to Ireland to meet me. There and then he offered me the job in Japan.

'It wasn't easy when I first arrived. A foreign woman in a strange country without any language ability whatsoever. I didn't even unpack for the first three months, but slowly things got better and I became more settled.

'Work-wise I have been allowed to do what I want, and I don't really know if I'm treated, or I should say thought of, as an equal by my Japanese male colleagues. It doesn't really matter so long as I can work and contribute to Canon in particular and society in general. But I think it's safe to say that they've accepted me. I'm certainly not mistreated.'

In general it seems that most foreign employees of Canon in Japan don't want to be treated as Japanese. In a way that is healthy, as Canon's directors claim they want to treat each national market as a unique venture, and meet local demands as they arise. Japanese employees, on the other hand, despite a few minor grumbles, seem extremely proud to be working for Canon, and though not believing true equality has yet been achieved, feel the company is on the right path.

As well as offering some of the best levels of sexual, intellectual and racial equality in Japan, Canon also prides itself on allowing a level of intellectual freedom that is perhaps the highest in Japan. But, we have to ask, is this purely a result of the necessity of attracting creative people, or does freedom form an integral part of company philosophy? As might be expected, Canon is not a paragon of freedom and liberality. How employees regard the levels of freedom they have depends on three major factors: age, sex and job description.

White-collar workers generally see themselves as relatively free compared with workers they know in other Japanese companies, and older employees consider themselves to be even more liberated than younger ones. Factory workers, on the other hand, just seem to want to get on with the job, and usually don't even consider freedom to be relevant to their work. The group that seems least satisfied with the amount of choice they have been given consists mainly of women.

Men in their twenties from Canon Inc. headquarters at Shimo-maruko were not overly impressed with Canon's claims to be leading the world in employee freedom. But even they had to admit that they had been given a reasonable level of choice. One said, 'The amount of freedom you get depends on which division you work in. In general business divisions and administration there isn't much freedom. You just follow orders. But in develop-ment areas it is probably much more. I think this is important. Many companies give up if a development doesn't bear fruit quickly, but Canon lets its researchers go on for much longer. This is a positive aspect of Canon culture. But from where I am, on the general staff, there isn't much freedom. Admittedly, it is a friendly and comfortable place to work, but when the chips are down and deadlines are coming, you can forget about free-dom. Just keep your head down and work.'

The second interviewee was slightly more positive. 'I think Canon workers get about the same freedom as employees in other companies as a rule. But when you are working on the development of something new you have a lot more freedom. There is also quite a wide choice allowed in the selection of the task you want to do or the product you want to work on.'

White-collar workers in their thirties were more positive still. One said, 'Getting on in Canon is not just a matter of dead-men's shoes. What makes the difference is the relationship one can have with one's bosses. Workers are allowed, even encouraged, to express their own ideas and opinions, and age is not seen as an inhibitor of openness.' A second employee in the same age group described his feelings on a purely personal level, saying, 'I have certainly been able to realize my own goals and express my opinions. In fact, the corporate culture in Canon encourages open discussion. In other words, there is a good level of intellectual freedom.'

White-collar males in their forties, now in middle management and facing the task of managing Canon in the early years of the next century, strongly believe they, and the company, have benefited from high levels of intellectual freedom and individual responsibility. One explained, 'When I first joined I was in the accounts department, so, as you would expect, there was not a lot of freedom or creativity. But when I was thirty I was sent to a loss-making subsidiary, where there was just the president and me. We had orders to turn it around. I learned then to think for myself and get on with the job in hand. After we'd achieved that, I was sent to another loss-making subsidiary and I turned that into a profitable concern. Practically all of my career has been spent in small subsidiaries and divisions where I have been left to get on with the job. Yes, I would definitely say I have had a lot of freedom.'

A second mid-career manager confirmed this belief. 'I've spent a lot of time in the development part of the business, and as Canon relies on these departments to prepare the products of the future, we have always had a lot of freedom. Top management never seemed to care if I was young, middle-aged or old, as long as I made a contribution, and I was free to decide what that contribution should be. Our research centres have even more freedom because they are developing the seeds of new businesses. During the past twenty years, as the company grew and grew, things may have gradually become a little more bureaucratic, but, when I talk to friends in other companies, I realize just how much freedom I had and still have.'

And a third concluded, 'One of the blessings of Canon is that it encourages employees to discuss things freely with their bosses. You don't just have to follow orders.' He did, however, express some concern about Japanese culture in general. 'When I was in America, I wasn't part of the mainstream of operations, but worked on my own and had to make all my own decisions. It was free and very enjoyable. But when I came back to Japan there was a problem. At first I continued to work in my American way, but eventually had to change to a more consensus style so that I didn't stick out too much from my colleagues. I prefer the American way, but you can't have everything.'

The blue-collar workers at the Ami plant looked at things very differently. One explained: 'Regarding freedom, you have to remember that this is a manufacturing plant, so individual opinions are not often listened to. In my case, I suppose I'm only about 80 per cent satisfied, because although I wanted to work in design I ended up in production. On the other hand, that's probably where my true talents lie.'

A second worker was slightly more positive. 'There are lots of things I'm not satisfied with but at least young people are listened to in Canon, and given the opportunity to develop their own styles and interests.' And a third summed up the feeling that, perhaps, most of the workers at Canon plants express privately. 'I'm not totally satisfied, but in Canon just about everything is open to negotiation and improvement, so I guess I'm not unhappy with my situation as a whole.'

Only the women, it seems, are far from satisfied. One said she felt trapped. 'I'm strictly limited in choice. I would like to see a change in the personnel system that would allow people like me to transfer to other jobs and departments.' A second was very specific about future problems she expects if Canon doesn't recognize everyone as an individual. 'Canon has been very successful developing hardware, but the market now is demanding more and more sophisticated software. The company needs to allow individuals of both sexes much more freedom and responsibility. Only then can we expect to get some really meaningful technological breakthroughs. There are too many conservative types at the top, however, and sometimes life is not easy.'

A third brought the matter of freedom down to the basic nuts and bolts of corporate relationships. When asked what she would like to change she replied, 'I'd like to change my boss. He's just too old-fashioned and it's impossible to get him to think in a modern way.'

It seems that some things never change, and the gap between the aspirations of men and women, young and old, white-collar and blue-collar, are universal. At least at Canon the problems have been identified and are being targeted for improvement. Just because the system is not yet perfect, say the directors, does not mean that they have nothing to be proud of.

CHAPTER SEVEN

'I wanted to quit. But pensions don't start until you're sixty-five, so I decided to stay.' Masahiro Tanaka was obviously thrilled when he learned he had been appointed president of Canon Europa in 1991. At fifty-seven, Tanaka, now senior managing director in charge of global marketing and chief of the Asia 15 Project, was the oldest person Canon had ever sent abroad for the first time. He adds with a laugh, 'I don't know why they chose me. Perhaps they just didn't want me over here.'

Modesty obviously stops Tanaka from admitting that Canon had chosen wisely. After joining the company in 1956, he had spent the next thirty-three years in the Camera Division where 'I did every job you could think of, and then some.' This understanding of all aspects of a business had in itself prepared him for the position. But that wasn't his only qualification. Between 1989 and 1991 he had been in the Corporate Planning Division and thus was in a good position to understand Canon's overall aims.

There is also the possibility that Canon wanted to round off Tanaka's abilities and experience in preparation for an even more important role back at headquarters. Director and Senior General Manager Yukio Yamashita, the man who built Canon UK into the success it is today, says, 'Canon has a habit of ensuring that the really important people have a thorough grounding in all aspects of the company, and internationalization is high on the agenda.'

It wasn't always that way. In the very early days of Canon's international development there weren't enough people actually to leave much of a choice. If your number came up, you went.

One of the first people Canon ever posted overseas, former Managing Director, now retired, Tomomasa Matsui, explains how the company started its international growth. 'In the very early post-war years Dr Mitarai studied just what the Occupation Force members bought in Japan to take home when they left. It wasn't much. About the only things they seemed interested in were pearls and silk. He decided to add cameras to the list, and though our advertising was only word-of-mouth, we were soon doing quite good business with direct sales to departing GIs. In fact, we were so successful in this field that Dr Mitarai concluded we should enter the domestic American market directly.

'With this in mind,' Matsui continues, 'he went to America on a fact-finding tour with the intention of sourcing a reliable and trustworthy distributor. It had to be a distributor. We just weren't strong enough financially, or organized enough internationally, to go it alone. Dr Mitarai had heard about Mr Charles H. Percy, the president of Bell & Howell, a major distributor, and planned to visit him. However, things didn't go quite according to plan. Just as Dr Mitarai arrived, Mr Percy left for a one-month honeymoon. There was nothing for him to do, but wait, and so he did.

'When Percy eventually returned, they met for discussions. Initially Dr Mitarai was disappointed. Percy admitted that the cameras were good products, and "would probably sell like hot cakes if they had a Made in Germany label". But, he added, Japan's image as a low-quality producer was so universally known, they couldn't be expected to take off very quickly.

'Percy suggested, in fact, that to help sales grow more quickly, Canon's cameras should be branded Bell & Howell. Dr Mitarai, while understanding the point being made, was not about to admit to anyone that Canon was second-best. He thanked Mr Percy, but explained that he preferred to keep the Canon name, saying he'd given birth to the baby and would prefer to nurture it himself.'

There was still one major obstacle the company had to surmount before it could really plan to expand overseas with any confidence. Matsui explains: 'Customers like Bell & Howell demanded a regular supply of cameras, which unfortunately Dr Mitarai didn't feel we could guarantee. The problem was simple. Our production plants were pre-war and of wooden construction. It was a miracle we hadn't lost everything during the wartime fire-bombing, but with peace there still wasn't security. The possibility of work stoppages through fire or other natural disasters was too strong to allow us accurately to estimate future production. If the plant burned down, how could we keep our promises? Therefore Dr Mitarai declined to make any guarantees he couldn't keep.

'While all this was going on, the land at Shimomaruko, now the company's headquarters, came on the market. Despite the fact that it was priced at ¥90 million [$249,307], and the company's net worth was only ¥50 million [$138,504], Dr Mitarai decided to go for it. His first move was to approach the banks, but at that time Japanese banks were almost as badly off as the rest of industry, and either couldn't, or wouldn't, lend Canon the money, except at extortionate interest rates. Unfortunately, there was no alternative and the loans were taken out. However, a white knight was just crossing the horizon. The giant Hong Kong-based trading company Jardine Matheson had been showing interest in acquiring worldwide distribution rights for Canon cameras and lenses. After considerable discussion, Dr Mitarai told them they could have the sales rights on the sole condition that they loaned Canon the money it needed at lower interest rates than the banks had given. Jardine agreed and made ¥180 million [$500,000], a staggering amount to us at the time, available. The Japanese banks were paid off and a much more reasonable repayment schedule for the Shimomaruko headquarters and plant site was agreed. The deal was good for both parties. Jardine sold a lot more of our products than we had expected, and with the extra income we paid back the loan in four years, a year ahead of schedule.'

The agreement with Jardine Matheson ran for several years with differing levels of success. After Canon's initial jubilation at having achieved a certain level of worldwide sales, the directors had to face the fact that Canon products were only a tiny part of the total range of products handled by the trading house. Eventually it was decided that a different way of selling overseas would have to be found, and the worldwide sales agreement with Jardine was allowed to lapse. In fact, Dr Mitarai decided that Canon should at least initially get on to the American market in a more direct way than by dealing through a Hong Kong-based company.

Matsui relates that 'ten years after Mitarai's first meeting with Percy, an agreement was reached with Bell & Howell. The Canon board, though, still felt that we should have some form of direct representation there. So in 1955, with the opening of the New York branch office, I was sent to America.

'But this wasn't the end of our problems. Despite our dreams, the New York branch was little more than a support centre for the marketing, and Bell & Howell was pulling the strings.'

As it turned out, Canon's initial optimism concerning the US market was ill-founded. The company faced many problems in its attempts to get a foothold. Not only were there still some quality-control problems with the products, but corporate finances were being stretched to the limit. The uphill struggle was made even harder because Canon was the last of the major Japanese camera manufacturers to enter the American market.

A brief history of the early years of Canon's New York adventure runs as follows. The New York branch was set up in

1955 to sell Model V cameras. They didn't sell as well as had been hoped – Americans thought they were cheaply made and not of satisfactory quality. In 1957, Canon NY made a net loss of $350,000 and considering that the company had already paid off a massive debt of $500,000 to Jardine Matheson three years earlier, this was considered much too much. Most staff were sent back to Japan and the sales office was mothballed. Local distributors took over all sales activities throughout the country and that is how things remained for about the next ten years.

In 1965, well after the Jardine Matheson loan had been paid off, and with things looking up in Japan, Canon launched the world's first ten-key electronic calculator. After considerable success in Japan, the next logical step for the Business Machine Division was the ever-growing US market. Canon therefore decided to try again. On 1 January 1966 Canon USA Inc. was resuscitated and started the business of selling calculators. At this time the young Fujio Mitarai, nephew of the founder, with only five years of experience in the company, was sent over to New York to study the camera market and prepare Canon for a successful re-entry.

Says Mitarai, now company president: 'Sending me to New York was quite logical. After joining Canon, I had worked for a year on the assembly line, and knew the products inside out. Then for two years I was in the Finance Department, which gave me a reasonable grounding in the money side of the business. This was followed by two years in the Domestic Sales Department, selling cameras to wholesalers. In other words, I was capable of applying what I knew to setting up a camera sales company in America.

'Unfortunately, I wasn't even allowed to get on with that. In the same year that we started with Canon New York, Canon in Tokyo went into economic crisis and the money needed for setting up a sales organization just didn't materialize. In other words, my main reason for being there had disappeared. All we could do was continue our distribution agreement with Bell & Howell for another six years, even though they had their own products and didn't really push ours enough. We were helpless.

'I was moved to accounting and personnel and spent the time until 1973 studying the market and preparing. By the time we were financially strong enough to go it alone and terminate the agreement with Bell & Howell, I was one of the best-prepared men ever seen. I was appointed head of the Camera Division, so I opened branches and hired staff.

'Even though things were finally on the move, because we'd wasted so many years, of the six Japanese camera makers selling in America, Canon had the smallest market share. We had to face the fact that we were relatively unknown. Ironically, considering that Americans had long been complaining about the low quality of Japanese goods, we also suffered because we made only top-quality, high-end cameras which weren't really popular. This meant that chain-store-type sales were out, so instead we went ahead and built a strong network of around 800 camera specialist outlets.

'Our first big break came in 1976 with the launch of the AE-1, the world's first computerized single-lens reflex [SLR] camera. The computerized central processing unit [CPU] was a break-through. Whereas cameras up until then had contained around 1,300 separate parts, the AE-1, because of its CPU, reduced this by about 300. It was therefore more reliable, and, perhaps more importantly, significantly cheaper. It reduced our selling price by between $100 and $150, a significant amount at that time. Sales began to grow.

'Even so, we were still only available through specialist stores and we had to face the fact the general public had little or no idea who we were and what we produced. I needed desperately to build our image. To do this we became the first Japanese camera maker ever to advertise on American television. It doesn't sound such a big deal now, but in those days it was epoch-making.

'The star we chose for our commercials was Australian tennis ace John Newcombe. We never regretted the choice. He was very easy to work with, popular, photogenic and, thankfully for us, more affordable than most of the home-grown American stars.

'The commercials really did it for us, and we recorded explosive sales figures for the next two years. By then we were the number one Japanese camera sales company in the US. And, as vice-president in charge of camera sales, I was proud, but ready to go home.

'By 1977 I'd been in the States for eleven years and was looking forward to returning to Japan. But, once again, things weren't to work out as I had expected. Mr Maeda, who was then president of both Canon Inc. and Canon Sales Co. Inc. in Japan, died suddenly, and Mr Seiichi Takikawa, currently chairman of Canon Sales Co. Inc., but then president of Canon USA, returned to Japan and took over Canon Sales Co. Inc.

'This, of course, meant that I couldn't leave America. Mr Hiroshi Suzukawa, vice-president of Canon Inc. in Tokyo, joined us as president, but stayed for less than two years. On 1 January 1979 I was appointed president of Canon USA Inc. and hunkered down for the long haul, which turned out to be another ten years.'

During this period, and for quite a few years after, Canon was growing at such a rate overseas that quite a lot of people, including Mitarai, had to stay abroad for extremely long periods. Another such case was that of Yukio Yamashita, now a director and senior general manager of personnel at headquarters, who spent so long in the UK that some people claim he is really British and has resorted to plastic surgery as a ploy to get ahead. Now in charge of selecting people to go overseas, and looking after them once they get there, Yamashita explains how he came to spend so long abroad.

'I spent twenty years, 1975 to 1995, in Europe, after only being in the company for thirteen years previous. I think the biggest reason I had to stay abroad was that we were expanding our operations and setting up our own sales organizations so quickly, that we had to take the if-it-ain't-broke-don't-fix-it attitude, and forget trying to rotate managers. I was told originally I would go for three years, but I became suspicious when I realized the person who'd made that promise had disappeared, so there were no guarantees.

'Actually the time I spent abroad was a very exciting time for me and for Canon. We only really began directly investing in our overseas distribution organizations in the early 1970s. Before that we had appointed a series of national distributors and did our business through them. As many companies have found, this can be a good way to get started in a foreign market, but no distributor can ever have the same passion for your products as you can. Therefore, and this is no reflection on any of our former distributors − in fact we took over most of them − we decided to change our policies and set up direct distribution routes.

'I first went to Holland, where I was the manager of the Electronic Data Processing Department. I worked there for three years and thought I would then be returning to Japan. At that time Canon Europa was going through some administrative changes and a serious reorganization, and the president asked me to stay and help for a couple more years.

'The reorganization and changes had been brought about by the problem of vastly differing performances in respective European national markets. When the company had set up Canon Europa, various assumptions, based on our Japanese and American experiences, had been made. Many of these proved to be untenable, and some downright impossible. The first mistake we made, of course, was to channel all European business through Canon Europa in Amsterdam. We simply hadn't realized the huge differences, both in culture and business styles, between the various countries of Europe. It was unreasonable of us to expect even the Dutch, perhaps the most internationalized of all races, to be able to understand and cater for all the national foibles of individual national markets. Our competitors had realized this and were going directly to each market. We were therefore trailing rather badly.

'The biggest mistake we made, however, was to treat all European countries as equals, offering the same prices to all our distributors. In a market like Japan, of course, this makes sense. But in Europe, the larger countries obviously have physically longer supply lines and often need to pay for extra warehousing, etc., just to keep the supply of products flowing. Therefore countries like France, Germany and the UK were being seriously outshone by, say, Belgium, Luxembourg and Switzerland.

'It didn't take us too long to realize that the smaller countries were not actually out-performing the larger ones. They were getting a much bigger bite of the profitability cherry because of their lower overheads. The answer to the problem was simple. While the current Amsterdam-oriented system could continue for the smaller markets, the larger countries would have to be allowed to deal directly with Canon Inc. in Tokyo. They would thus be able to work out the deals best suited to their individual markets. This was all very well and good on paper. But in reality it was much more difficult to achieve than it first appeared.'

The problem that Yamashita is describing is one that the Japanese hardly ever seem to solve to a satisfactory degree. In Japanese business, as in politics and society in general, almost everything follows a system of unwritten, but mutually under-stood, rules. Combine this with language difficulties, and at that time it would have been almost impossible to accommodate a sudden increase in non-Japanese dealing directly with Tokyo. To put it bluntly, there simply weren't enough English-speakers at Canon Inc. in Tokyo to make such a system work.

Yamashita continues: 'The only answer to the problem was to employ many more Japanese throughout Europe in coordinating roles. Though the ultimate aim was to train locals and replace the Japanese with them eventually, as a first move there was no other choice but to bring over more Japanese from Tokyo, and to ask those already there to stay longer.

'The new system, therefore, was to have Japanese in administration and managerial roles for several years while they trained the locals. This would also allow Tokyo time to train up enough people to eventually handle the European set-up in English. In 1981, we started with an independent company in France. This was followed by the UK in 1982 and Germany the following year. By this time I had been abroad for five years and was expecting to be sent back to Tokyo after completing my part in organizing the new system. I was slightly surprised, therefore, to be asked to go over and run Canon UK for a couple of years. However, it was a challenge, and I was still only forty-one, so I accepted with pleasure. The couple of years eventually turned into almost fifteen, but that's life.'

When he arrived in the UK, Yamashita found that he had to learn yet another style of corporate culture, but he says he settled in very quickly despite this, and soon came to love his new position. He explains: 'When I moved to the UK, I found it so different from Holland. I was shocked. Canon Europa, in the early eighties, was very much a Japanese organization. To some extent it still is. At that time the managing was done by Japanese, and the local Dutch staff were in junior positions. In the UK, however, we already had several Britons in senior management positions. These included Martin Laws, who is now the managing director.

'He was already working there as financial controller when I joined. When I arrived, the company was not performing well and the employees were confused. It wasn't their fault. The main reason was that we had a joint managing directorship. That in itself is not necessarily bad. But we hadn't even limited the position to two; we had three supposedly equal joint managing directors. One was Japanese and the other two were British. On paper it seemed to make sense. The Japanese would be in charge of liaison with Tokyo; one of the Britons would take care of the copier business, and the other would look after our calculator sales. As I say, it looked good on paper, but in reality it was a disaster. The Japanese man, instead of being seen as the point man for Japanese liaison, was regarded as a Tokyo spy. Everyone believed he was watching over them and reporting everything back to headquarters. Morale was very low, and there was very much an us-and-them attitude.

'It would have been worse if we had been dealing with cameras as well. Perhaps we would have had a fourth joint managing director. But luckily I had a year before we took over the camera business from the distributors. This gave me the time to plan and reorganize.

'My aim was eventually to replace myself with a non-Japanese. But, although we had several good prospective managing directors, nobody had yet been really tested. So the first thing I did was to set up a management committee. From this team I hoped to choose the eventual directors, but because it was a committee, I was able to judge each candidate over a period of time. This meant that I did not have to promote anyone to director level before I was certain of his or her long-term potential. It also resulted in enabling me to remove some people from the management team as and when their performance didn't meet my expectations.'

Despite Yamashita's plans for bringing locals into top

management, he was not really optimistic about being able to promote a Briton quickly to the very top position. Being a realist, he knew that there would be some resistance to such a move. For example, he realized that the annual global managers' meeting could be a problem. This conference of Canon managers from all around the world is a major aspect of Canon's international management. Each year, for two weeks in October, senior managers from all over the world descend on Tokyo for a round of new product seminars, training sessions, briefings and debriefings, and strategy planning. Yamashita says: 'When we had a top management world conference, if everybody was Japanese there was no problem. But, if one of the participants was foreign, the entire proceedings would have to take place in English. I expected strong resistance to such a move.'

It apparently hadn't occurred to Canon that it would be possible to use an interpreter to allow the non-Japanese to understand what was going on and to contribute, even if the meetings were held in Japanese. Even in the most enlightened Japanese mind, there is still a strong belief that the Japanese language simply cannot be translated into other languages. Such myths are rife in Japan and do much more damage to international relations than is normally credited.

In this case, however, eventually, after almost fifteen years, when Yamashita finally did return to Japan, he was replaced by the Briton Martin Laws. Yamashita explains why he thinks it finally happened. 'Canon globally has many non-Japanese top executives. Worldwide we have 143 companies and more than half have non-Japanese directors, but most are not dealing directly with Canon Inc. In Europe, for example, the majority of subsidiaries and affiliates use Canon Europa as a clearing-house for contact with Tokyo. Only the larger organizations, France, the UK, Germany, deal direct. I thought this would mean that the top job would remain in Japanese hands. But when Mr Fujio Mitarai took over as president

17 Canon cameras and lenses taking an active role at the tennis tournament in Flushing Meadows, Queens, New York, 1995.

18 In 1977 Canon moved into celebrity product endorsement, featuring tennis star John Newcombe in Canon USA's AE-1 television and print advertisements.

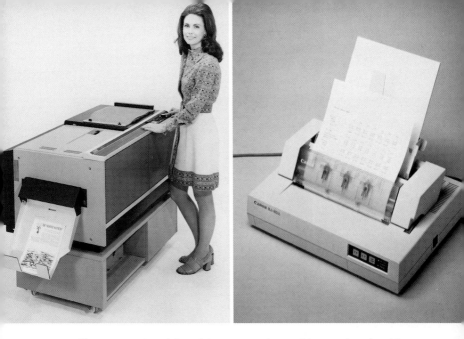

19 The NP-1100, Japan's first plain-paper copying machine, was introduced in 1970.

20 The BJ-80, Canon's first Bubble Jet Printer, was introduced in 1985.

21 The LBP-10, the world's first compact-sized laser beam printer, was introduced in 1979.

22 The top management at the fiftieth anniversary celebrations in 1987. *From left to right*, Fujio Mitarai (president since 1995), Hajime Mitarai (president, 1993-5), Ray Templin (service manager for consumer products service division, Canon USA) and Ryuzaburo Kaku (president, 1977-89, chairman since 1989). Mr Templin was invited to the ceremony as the non-Japanese employee representative because he had served the company longest. They are wearing *happi*, a traditional Japanese workman's livery, and are breaking open a sake cask in a traditional Japanese celebration ceremony.

23 President Ryuzaburo Kaku announces the *kyosei* philosophy in 1988 with the launch of the First Global Corporation Plan.

24 Ryuzaburo Kaku (*third from left*) attending the Caux Round Table at Guandong Province, South China in 1993. He belongs to this Swiss-based organization that includes business leaders from the United States, Japan and Europe.

25 Keizo Yamaji (president, 1989–93; vice–chairman, 1993–6) at the commencement ceremony at Christopher Newport University, Virginia, USA. He received an honorary doctorate in science at the ceremony (1993). *From left to right*: Richard Summerville, Provost for Christopher Newport University, Dr Keizo Yamaji, Dr Anthony Santoro, president of CNU, and Allan Witt, Rector of the Board of Visitors. The university is situated near Canon's manufacturing plant in Virginia.

26 The Canon Ecology R&D Centre opened in 1993 in Kizu, a small community near Kyoto. Scientists work on harnessing energy from the sun and pursuing the 'clean energy' ideal. Solar cell panels are seen as a promising source of clean energy for the future.

27 Japan's Emperor and Empress with Dr Hajime Mitarai at the ceremony of the Imperial Invention Prize in 1994. A group of researchers from Canon received an award from the Japan Institute for Invention and Innovation for their work on bubble jet printing technology.

28 Ryuzaburo Kaku is presented with the BS7750 certificate from the chairman of the Société Génerale de Surveillance (SGS), Elizabeth Salina Amorini, in 1995. By the end of 1996, twenty-one Canon plants worldwide had received the international standard for environmentally responsible production.

29 Fujio Mitarai and Hewlett-Packard President Lewis E. Platt unveiling a rock with the word *kyosei* carved on it, at Canon headquarters in Shimomaruko, 1996. It refers to their 'loyal friendship and a commitment to excellence'.

共生

*Inspired by a loyal friendship
and a commitment to excellence,
Canon and Hewlett-Packard
leading the world in the family of
LaserJet printers*

*Great Relationship Celebration
April 1996*

30 Richard Burke (*third from right*), chairman of the Canon Foundation, talking to professors from Holland and Japan. One of the main activities of the Foundation is the fellowship programme for professors of the two countries.

31 Former US Ambassador Walter Mondale with Dr Fujio Mitarai at the new president's reception in February 1996.

32 A view of the Fuji-Susono Research Park, a facility in Shizuoka prefecture at the foothills of Mount Fuji, opened in October 1996. It is designed to house all of the company's R&D operations related to electronic photography.

things changed. He had spent over twenty years in America and, like me, was eager to internationalize. Therefore, when the question of a new managing director for the UK came up, Martin was our first choice.'

Canon may be taking something of a lead in the appointing of non-Japanese to top positions in foreign subsidiaries and affiliates, but is it as open in the appointment of foreigners to genuine top positions? Usually, in Japan, the only time foreigners ever get appointed to the boards of Japanese companies is when those companies are in dire straits and all channels of Japanese help have been tried and exhausted. A recent example of this is the appointment of an American as president of Mazda, the car manufacturer. In this case, Ford already held a considerable share in the ailing Japanese auto manufacturer, and when it came to the crunch, merely upped its interest and took over. Another example was when an electronic manufacturer was near bankruptcy several years ago. No Japanese saviour could be found, so the company was eventually sold to Polly Peck – not a particularly good move as things turned out. On the other hand, when American investor T. Boone Pickens demanded a place on the board of a Toyota affiliate, he was stonewalled into defeat. Even though he was the single largest stockholder, he wasn't allowed even the slightest say in the future of the company. All the other stockholders stayed together and presented a complete cold shoulder. So how does Canon stand on the matter of non-Japanese board members?

Yamashita says, 'Gradually, the conditions for a non-Japanese main board member will occur. It is only natural as our operations abroad are almost bound to grow faster than in Japan. When this has happened, there will be no escaping the fact that we will need international input at the board level. I don't think it's a matter of if; it's more a question of when. But it won't be easy for either the Japanese or the foreigners.

'The main problem will be cultural, not linguistic. In Japan we are very much group-oriented. Gradually individualism is taking more part, but management decision-making is almost always still done in the traditional Japanese way – in groups. I can understand the difficulties and frustrations the non-Japanese are going to experience. I really learned my management techniques in Europe, not in Japan. When I eventually came home I was confused, to say the least. Decision-making is so complicated and slow in Japan. I have to pay so much attention to so many areas. I've gradually got used to it, I suppose, but my staff still have to keep a close eye on me to make sure I follow all the rules. I don't know how a non-Japanese will take to this.'

Yamashita may have his doubts, but also says that the Japanese are finally beginning to realize that the world is not merely divided into Japanese and non-Japanese. He says that many people are starting to see that there are differences between other individual countries as well. He was surprised, for example, when he moved from Holland to the UK and found himself in a totally different culture.

'I was very shocked,' he explains. 'I found there are more differences between the Dutch and the British than there are between the British and the Japanese. This may partly be because of the peculiarity of Canon Amsterdam, but that isn't all. The Dutch are more straightforward. They come to work at nine and they leave at five-thirty. During that time they'll get on with their work, and if they have a problem, they'll tell you.

'The British, on the other hand, are less direct. You have to do many things in a much less formal way, just like in Japan. Whereas in Holland, if I stayed after five-thirty, I'd be either on my own or with a group of other Japanese, in England, when the working day was officially over, quite a lot of people would start filtering into my office. Then the suggestion for "a quick half" would be made, and we'd all go down to the local pub. It was at these times that many of our management problems were solved and team relationships cemented.'

This feeling of being comrades and friends as well as associates is also experienced by the British who knew Yamashita in England. Managing Director Martin Laws explains: 'Yukio Yamashita was always known just as Mr Y, and he is the one who really made Canon UK what it is today. He had the talents we were badly lacking before his arrival. He had a long-term view of the markets and was a strategic planner. He treated us as his friends and was definitely seen as our friend. He has a very nice way of never apparently giving straight orders, but nevertheless always getting his way. Now, that's good management. In many ways, we never thought of him as a Japanese. He was a Brit, just like the rest of us.'

One of Canon's strengths seems to be that they have chosen well, or luckily, in the people they have sent abroad. Equally they have been fortunate in finding not only people who adapt to foreign countries, but also senior managers who have been willing to stay abroad for decades. Yamashita says that keeping people overseas for decade after decade has never been a Canon policy. It is simply that the company was growing so fast that it would have been impossible to rotate them. Company policy, he says, is for staff members to work overseas for four to five years before returning to Japan. It is questionable whether this is the right policy. Certainly the Japanese sent to Europe and America have earned places in the hearts of the locals that many Japanese company directors would be extremely jealous of.

Most of the Canon board members believe it is necessary to understand different cultures, and feel that keeping expatriates in place for long periods has distinct advantages. President Fujio Mitarai says, 'Businesses exist in a relationship with the customs and traditions of the country or countries in which they operate. American methods, while being perfect for America, don't necessarily work in Japan.

'The United States has a very versatile and mobile work-force and can make strong demands on the employees. Japan, on the other hand, has to follow a tradition of strict seniority in a system of lifetime employment. In America the education system nurtures individuals and leaders: that's why there are many successful people as well as a lot of dropouts. But America has room even for the dropouts. It has a land mass twenty-six times that of Japan, but has only just under twice Japan's population. If we were to introduce the excessively competitive American-style society into Japan, society would crack under the pressure.

'I think we have to plan globally but act locally. Fairness doesn't belong to one nationality. It is an international concept. When I look at each independent Canon subsidiary, I want them to remain independent and do the best they can for their own countries.'

Haruo Murase, president of Canon USA Inc., who has lived in the United States and Canada for twenty-six years, adds, 'Canon USA has the aim of fitting in with the communities we serve. We work on a local level and try to do what is right by our communities. For example, many Japanese companies are not accustomed to charity, because they simply don't understand what it is. In Japan, charity is thought to be the same as begging. In America, of course, donating to charity is seen as not only acceptable but socially responsible. Naturally, we give to charity.'

The level to which Murase has fitted in with American ways is strongly demonstrated by his relationships with employees. Even at the top management level Canon USA reflects the broad spectrum of ethnic origins so typical of America, but undreamt of in mono-ethnic Japan. All the employees I talked to said that the question of nationality never came up, either in management's reaction to them or in their relations with executives. I was told that in the Canon USA family an employee is judged purely on ability and not in any way by ethnicity.

Thus fitting in with the local community goes even beyond the obvious Canon family loyalty. After interviewing President Murase, I was taking a cab back to my hotel. The taxi driver asked me where I'd been. I told him that I'd been interviewing the president and CEO of Canon USA, to which the driver replied, 'He's a good guy. Not like a Japanese at all. He's just like one of us. He came to the school my son goes to to give out some prizes and when we met him it was just like talking to another American. Yeah, he's OK.' Praise indeed.

Journalist Toru Arai agrees with Canon's way of doing things. 'Most Japanese feel that working abroad is only a very temporary move, and therefore try not to commit themselves to their adopted country but to keep in touch with everything that is going on at HQ. At Canon, however, though the majority of workers feel that they will no doubt return to Japan at some point, they expect to be abroad for a long time. This helps to foster the belief that Canon is a company working on a truly global scale.'

His thoughts are backed up by Dr Roderich Graf von Stomm, the president of both Canon Austria and Canon East Europe, himself a German who has been living in Austria for over twenty years. 'Canon's greatest strength is its localization and commitment to stability. Look over there,' he says, pointing to the logo of a leading copier competitor on top of a nearby office block. 'They change their executive officers every two or three years, and send over new ones from head office. Personally I think it's great, because I know that by the time they understand the market and are in a position actually to do something innovative or intelligent, they will be on the plane out of the country, and another learner will take over.'

Even Canon executives have to admit, however, that spending years and years abroad does have its down side. But, they say, most of the problems are personal, not business-related. Yamashita says, 'I have a wife and two daughters. When I left Japan, the elder was ten and the younger five. The younger girl started at the American school in Amsterdam and had no problems at all. When she moved to London she switched to a local school and then went on to college in England. With the elder, however, I made a mistake. I'd thought I was going to come back to Japan, so after four years I sent her back to my mother's house, so she could get back into the Japanese education system. When I found out I was actually staying in Europe, I brought her back, but she was already out of step with the British education system. It was very hard for her to adjust.

'When I came back to Japan my children were fine, but I had a serious problem getting used to the long daily commute. Nowadays I leave home at six-thirty and still the train is over-crowded. I spend just over an hour travelling each way. In England I only had a ten-minute commute. That was the life.'

Some Canon staff may have difficulty readjusting to Japan, but they certainly seem to have solved the problem of fitting in abroad. So how does Canon select its expatriates? Mitarai explains: 'Even at the time when I was sent to work in America Canon did not choose people to go abroad because of age, position or seniority. We selected people then, and still do, by studying our employees and seeing who we feel will best be able to achieve our goals in a specific job in a particular company. And that, of course, means that the selected person must be happy to go, or those goals will never be achieved.

'It is true that some of Canon's people, including me, with twenty-three years in America, have stayed in their adopted countries for a very long time. But the length of stay depends on many factors, not the least of which is the individual employee's willingness to stay. I first went to the US as an accountant and stayed because the company was growing so quickly, and, as I learned more about the market, I was better able to function than a replacement would have been.

'I genuinely feel that if you want to achieve something in a country other than your own you need to stay at least ten years. If a person is competent and willing, we should ask him or her to consider ten years rather than the shorter term of five, which is official company policy.

'Sometimes our choices may not appear logical on the surface. For example, Mr Katayama in Canon Europa could at first sight look like a fish out of water. He's been a life-long engineer in Japan and he's now been put in a marketing position in a foreign country. But this is not as illogical as it may sound. His job is to restructure the Canon Europa company and prepare it for the future and even more independence from Tokyo. Who better than an engineer to organize a restructuring? We also have to consider his own future. He is an important member of our management team, and in a period that is demanding more and more internationalization, he hadn't previously had any international experience. Therefore we thought he'd be in a much better position to contribute to Canon's global future after he had experienced life and work in an international environment.'

Katayama concurs. 'I think being transferred here to Europe has been good for me. Now that I have experienced the differences in various national customs, I feel that my vision has been widened and my way of thinking globalized. I hope that throughout the remainder of my career I will be able to continue to contribute to the global localization of Canon. This, of course, depends on the extent to which I can successfully globalize myself.'

Finding the right people to go abroad, however, is not always easy. And, says Yamashita, it is getting tougher. 'It is much more difficult nowadays to get younger Japanese to live abroad. Because it is much easier nowadays than it used to be to go on foreign trips, many people don't actually want to go and live abroad. They see it as a bad career move. They are afraid of losing good contacts. In the past it was different. Nobody would refuse, but nowadays we really have to convince them.

'We now have to sweeten the package a little if we send people to some countries, particularly less developed states, like those in Asia. This is to compensate them for lower standards of living in those countries. But, of course, this doesn't apply to Europe or America. There are still plenty who want to go there.'

Perhaps one of the reasons why Japanese staff members don't mind living abroad for long periods, particularly in Western, developed countries, is that when overseas they have much more freedom to get their teeth into practical business matters and make real decisions. Yamashita says, 'When I was in the UK I didn't have to consult with Tokyo except for very big investments. Up to about £12 million [$19.68 million], I just made my own decisions. Even when I decided to sponsor the English professional Football League I didn't have to ask for permission. Martin and I made the decision. And that cost us around £10 million [$16.4 million]. Tokyo found out when the news was trumpeted all round the world, but they didn't think I'd done wrong.'

Katayama of Canon Europa adds, 'President Mitarai understands that Canon needs to become a truly global company with total understanding of individual markets. He also sees that if Canon is to succeed better than any other company, the different areas or countries must be given their own heads and be allowed to be run with local management and employees.

'It is true that right now Canon's activities are still controlled by Tokyo to a certain extent, although even now this may be less than with other Japanese companies. In the future, however, we are aiming to make each area of the globe an equal partner in the business. We will therefore see strategic planning for Asia, Europe, America and Japan.'

Canon UK's Martin Laws says, 'Canon has always had a

commitment to localization. Compared with the American company I used to work for, with Canon I get much more freedom to get on with my job. If I want advice, it is there, but I have never been ordered to take one specific action instead of another. I'm left to get on with it.' Canon USA's Murase adds, 'I have two main functions in this company. First I act as a liaison between the parent company in Tokyo and the US side of our enterprise. This is not generally the way one may expect it, and doesn't mean that I only funnel orders from Tokyo to America. My other task is to get our corporate message over to our employees. It is not just a matter of orders but, rather, helping people understand why something is being done. And by doing it, we can expect more understanding and loyalty. I suppose it would be best to describe both of my functions as bridge-building.'

Dr Stomm in Austria agrees. 'When this company was formed it was run from Geneva. But this changed over the next few years and by the time I took over in 1985, it was much more of a national company.

'When, for example, the barriers dividing Europe fell in 1989, it was obvious that Austria was seen as the centre for the new potential markets. Masahiro Tanaka, then head of Canon Europa, decided to set up a completely new company to deal with the developing markets in central Eastern Europe.

'Canon East Europe was formed and I was put in charge. I make my own decisions without constantly having to refer to Tokyo, or even Amsterdam. For example, one evening a few years ago, I was one of the few people left in the offices as it was getting quite late. I was looking out of my office window down towards the car park, when I saw an old car with a refrigerator strapped to the roof enter the lot. A youngish man dressed in casual clothes and tennis shoes got out and started banging on the door.

'As almost everyone had already left, I went down to investigate and let him in. He explained that he was on the way back home to Poland and wanted to become a Canon dealer in his home country. Luckily, our export manager was still in the building, so I put the two of them together, and in practically no time at all they had reached agreement on terms.

'That young man is now our biggest dealer in Poland, and when he visits us now, he drives a top-of-the-range Mercedes. Canon gave me the freedom to make a choice without hamstringing me with unnecessary bureaucracy, and it paid off.'

Freedom is definitely better than the alternative, but, says Yamashita, Canon is not yet in a position to say that it has got everything right. 'Decentralization could still be a problem. Even though in general it is very good that each subsidiary can develop its own policies, if we were to need integration at some time in the future, we might not be able to achieve it.

'Unless the foreign managers and directors are put on an equal footing with the Japanese, we will never truly be able to achieve independence, and, even worse, may not be able to stay integrated as a group. At present we have 76,000 people working for Canon. Of these 50 per cent are in Japan. We have 1,000 Japanese working overseas as coordinators and managers, etc. That means 1,000 Japanese out of 38,000 employees, a ratio of one Japanese to every 38 employees, is working outside Japan. This is too high. We will continue to need expatriate employees, but, as in other non-Japanese multinationals, the expatriates should not come from a single country. If the best person to manage India, for example, is a Briton, he or she should be sent. If the most suitable manager for Holland is Italian, then that person should be selected.

'We are beginning this process. For example, we are currently looking to recruit ten people from Ireland, where the universities are willing to cooperate with companies. We will bring these ten to Japan for at least a year, to learn the semiconductor business. They will then go back to Europe and will be assigned to different countries. They will be regarded as international staff and do the jobs that used to be done only by Japanese. That is the beginning of our next stage of development.'

So Canon may not yet have achieved their goal of internationalization, but, unlike many Japanese competitors, they seem to be aware of the problems they are facing. And that, perhaps, is half the battle.

CHAPTER EIGHT

In the earliest periods of Japan's animistic pre-history Fuji-san (Mount Fuji) was revered as the home of the gods – a Japanese Mount Olympus, in fact. Even today, both Japan's major religions, Shintoism (indigenous ancestor worship) and Buddhism, regard the mountain as sacred. Until 1888 women, considered unclean because of the menstrual cycle, were banned from setting foot on it. As early as the eighth century, Akahito Yamabe, one of Japan's foremost poets, was writing verses in praise of its beauty. And probably the strongest symbol of Japan in the minds of most foreigners is the series of woodblock prints, *Views of Fuji*, by Hokusai (1760–1849).

It is difficult not be awed by the magnificence of Fuji's classic volcano contours, rising as the mountain does from a necklace of small lakes to a snow-capped peak, 3,776 metres (12,389 feet) above. Japanese and foreigners alike still seek the spirituality of a Fuji-san view when looking for inspiration or serenity. And the people at Canon are no different. Some of them, however, are considerably luckier than most.

Two of the main buildings of Canon's Fuji-Susono Research Park, which opened in October 1996, are connected by an elevated walkway. When visitors arrive at the centre, the first thing they see is a magnificent view of Fuji-san, framed as in a photograph by the walls of the two buildings to the left and right, the walkway at the top and the ground at the bottom. A Japanese camera manufacturer could not possibly have come up with a better image for one of its major development facilities.

GLOBAL RESPONSIBILITIES AND LOCAL DECISIONS

Fuji-Susono Research Park is home to 1,000 of Canon's leading researchers, working mainly in areas connected to electro-photography, a core Canon technology with applications in over 70 per cent of the company's products. Few companies, Japanese or non-Japanese, could have designed such a centre. Fewer would have taken so much care to minimize the effect on the natural environment, and fewer still would have bothered to take all this trouble just to harness Japan's most famous beauty spot to the development of individuality and creativity.

Teruo Suzuki, deputy general manager of the General Affairs Division, says, 'All of the rooms where seminars, meetings and discussions take place, as well as rest areas, cafeterias and canteens, are on the side facing Mount Fuji. We believe that the serenity of the view will bring peace of mind and thereby stimulate the creative juices.'

Since the centre is still very new, it remains to be seen whether Fuji-san with its semi-religious tranquillity will nurture the creative genius that will be necessary for Canon to maintain its strength and dominance into the coming century. But the concept is not new. The company has already proved that ambiance is well worth the money invested when designing and building research facilities. Most of Canon's other R&D centres are also located in beautiful, pastoral areas, and have been remarkably successful over the past twenty years or so.

R&D Headquarters Canon Research Center is located near Atsugi City, physically close to Tokyo but culturally and environmentally a million miles away. Once again, as at Fuji-Susono, the facility is approached along a steeply rising road that meanders through luxurious oak forests and provides occasional panoramic views of beautiful countryside and lush farmland. As the visitor steps from the car and takes a breath of the deliciously fresh air, the first thing he or she sees are three pillars supporting the entranceway. Each of these pillars is inscribed with one of the philosophical pillars of Canon research and corporate culture, the Three Js, *ji-hatsu, ji-kaku* and *ji-chi* (self-motivation, self-awareness and self-management).

To the Western mind, this may all seem to be so much pseudo-religious mumbo-jumbo, but there is no doubt that it works in Japan, at least for Canon. While working here at Atsugi as manager, Ichiro Endo, now managing director and chief executive of Product Development Headquarters, made the quantum leap, in research and design terms, that ensured Canon's success over the past fifteen or so years, and is partially guaranteeing its future profitability. In Canon and throughout Japan, Ichiro Endo is known as Mr Bubble Jet.

During the extremely long gestation period of the Bubble Jet printing technology, Endo needed not only a firm belief in the Three Js, but also the certainty that, however long it took, Canon would keep faith with him and continue to fund the research. He had both.

Endo has worked for Canon for over thirty years and is a very strong supporter of the kind of intellectual freedom that is at the core of the company's philosophy. The development of the technology for the Bubble Jet Printer (BJP) is just one of the many examples where Canon went out on a limb but came back safely with the fruit. Endo describes the BJP development process: 'Canon, of course, started with cameras, but in the sixties we diversified into copiers with the development of New Process [NP] plain paper copier technology. This then became a core business, and, following the natural course of things, after it had been successfully developed and commercialized, it moved out of the realm of R&D. Once this had happened, in the late seventies, we researchers had to look for new areas of technology to develop.

'We studied various fields, including the development of new recording technologies and the possible production of post-electrophotography. On a personal level, I looked around at what I thought was interesting, and decided there was considerable potential in the research and development of ink jet printing technology.

'However, before you can even turn your mind to a new business venture, you have to make sure you're not wasting your time or simply duplicating someone else's prior research. My first job, then, was to survey all the existing patents regarding ink jet printing technology. At Canon we don't like to imitate, and we certainly don't want to infringe other companies' patents. So before we can begin to develop a new area of technology, we need to know exactly where we stand with regard to existing patents.

'My project was just one of several that the R & D teams were working on in the late seventies, when Dr Hajime Mitarai took over as head of research. The main themes were as follows:

1. Bubble Jet technology. This was code-named DOG, from D for Digital, the type of technology in question.
2. Future camcorder technology, code-named FOX (F for Future).
3. Small systems for laser-beam printers, code-named SHEEP (S for Small).
4. Canon automatic typewriters, code-named CAT (C for Canon, A for automatic, and T for typewriters).

'I was the head of the DOG team but can claim no credit for the name. Dr Mitarai loved codes, so he chose the project names.

'The process of research and development wasn't easy, and I feel that few companies would have had the faith and patience to see it through. It took us a long, long time to develop the BJP line, and we were often near defeat. But we persevered. Sometimes the breakthroughs came almost as accidents, but luckily for us, they always occurred in time to give us fresh hope.

I believe that, like giving birth, if your project's labour pains are long and the delivery is difficult, the chances are you'll produce a beautiful baby. Or at least you'll appreciate what you have given life to much more than if everything had gone easily. The LBP was such a baby, but in the past twenty years it has grown into a gorgeously adult annual business worth about ¥100 billion [$0.8 billion].

'My first real job, once the decision to go ahead had been made, was to set up the DOG team. To do this we dissolved several other project groups and selected an original staff of around forty. It was a truly multitalented group, and so it had to be, as we were starting the project from scratch. At first, though, even the choice of people caused us some teething problems. We had a lot of brilliant people working in a very narrow area of research, which inevitably resulted in a certain amount of dissatisfaction, with people treading on each other's toes. It took us some time, in fact until the programme was really expanding, before the team was really able to gel.

'When we had finally assembled the DOG team, our primary task was to decide what form of ink jet technology we were going to develop. There are two types: continuous drop and drop on demand. The former is very complex and has the disadvantage of having constantly to capture and then recycle the ink. On the positive side, though, it has the distinct technical advantage in that the flow of ink only has to be started once. Although no products using this technology were then available, a great deal of research had been carried out by other companies, and many patents had already been filed.

'The alternative system, drop on demand, is simpler, at least in theory. Because the ink is only released when needed, there is no need to develop a constant recycling system. The problem here, of course, was designing a simple and maintenance-free method of starting and stopping the flow. As with the continuous drop system, many patents had already been registered for this technology by our competitors. Even so, we decided to try this route.

'I often think that success in science is just as much a matter of realizing the importance of your mistakes as being able to predict what will happen in your experiments. As in many other cases, the first major breakthrough in BJP development came as the result of a totally unintentional occurrence. During one experiment, a soldering iron we were using came accidentally in contact with a syringe holding ink. When the hot iron touched the tip of the needle, the expansion caused a perfect droplet of ink to be released. When I saw what had happened, I realized the potential. It was at this moment that the BJP was actually born, even though it took us several more years to conclude the development.

'This happy accident made me consider the possibility of combining ink jet technology with a thermal capillary system. As luck would have it, they were working on electronic calculators in the laboratory next door, so I asked them to lend us some thermal heaters and a selection of 100-micron hollow fibres. The theory I came up with is simple. The fibres are filled with ink, and when the ink is needed a signal is sent to the heater. The capillary fibre is then heated and each cell releases a perfect droplet of ink. The fibre, therefore, simply works as a nozzle.

'As with most projects, though the theory was simple, making it work was much more difficult. We came up against many problems, and began to understand why other companies had long ago abandoned this line of research. For example, controlling the heat in a 100-micron fibre was unbelievably difficult. If it got too hot, the ink burned, and the gooey residue thus formed would gum up the heater and stop it working. We were just about at the end of our tether with this problem and near to giving up, when the obvious answer was suggested. We decided not to use existing inks, but develop our own, specially for the BJP. And this is what we did, with the bonus of adding even more value to the eventual product.

'Another problem we faced concerned erosion. Inks are water-based, and as each drop came in contact with the electrode that drove the heater, the electrode became eroded. A system of passivation to stop such erosion had to be invented. This took us another couple of years to develop and again increased our harvest of patents.

'Then there were the constant heater breakdowns we suffered. Each time a bubble burst and a droplet of ink was released, it caused a minor cavitation shock. Eventually these millions of shocks simply caused the heater to fail. We therefore had to come up with even more patents for a heater motor that could withstand cavitation shock.

'Eventually, however, we overcame the major problems. But even then each day seemed to bring a host of minor snags. Looking back on the project, I'm amazed we ever managed to carry it through. But, I suppose, with such a multitalented team, and with the total support of Canon throughout the years of development, success was inevitable.'

Looking back on what can perhaps be regarded as Canon Research Center's finest hour, it would be more than a little mean-minded to begrudge Endo his sense of glory. According to Hideharu Takemoto, president of Canon Sales Co. Inc., the development of the BJP was crucial to the sales expansion of the Canon group. 'Probably the most important product group in terms of helping growth for the recent years was that of printers. This year, for example, Canon Sales Co. is responsible for 40 per cent of Apple Computer sales in Japan, as well as 20 per cent of IBM PC sales. This has only been possible because, with the synergy of our printer range, we can offer a complete and attractive package.' But the development of the bubble jet was almost two decades ago. As this century winds down, Canon needs to ask itself whether it has anyone capable of carrying the company through to the technology of the twenty-first century.

In fact, the company has already faced up to the problems of the future, or so it claims, and the current senior general manager of the Research Center, Dr Takashi Nakagiri, believes, with some reservations, that Canon is well situated to develop the technologies and products that will be needed.

He explains: 'The role of this centre is to develop new technologies that will carry Canon profitably into the next century. We are currently working in areas such as long-term memory, tera-bit memory, optical LAN devices, large-screen flat displays and bioremediation, many of which, though now in the early stages of development, will have huge effects on the way we will live in the coming decades.

'Our mission is to nurture the seeds for the future crops of Canon technologies. The technology for our biggest recent individual success, the Bubble Jet Printer, was born here, when Ichiro Endo was the manager, and we expect to be able to follow successfully in his footsteps. We are now looking at technologies that will supersede the BJP.

'We have a hard row to hoe, because in Japan companies have to cover all aspects of research. In many Western countries, a great deal of basis research is done at universities, but that doesn't really happen over here. Our education system is such that we can't expect any creative thinking to emerge, so all must be done on a corporate level. And that is where the importance of the intellectual freedom we have in Canon comes to the fore.

'Our aim at this research centre, and at all other Canon facilities, is to avoid mainstream thinking. We want people to think for themselves and, in a manner of speaking, create new technological realities from their fantasies. We can only expect this to happen if we respect the independence and freedom of our researchers and let them work in areas they enjoy and are enthused by. They, on the other hand, will only be successful if they maintain very high levels of self-discipline.

'This may sound a little like a contradiction, but it isn't really. However, to ensure high levels of researcher self-discipline, there is one cardinal rule that everyone must follow. We demand that each and every researcher files at least four patents a year. We don't stipulate in which areas they must file, only that they must do it in one area or another.

'Remember that patents today have to be taken out on even the most minor processes, so if a researcher is on his or her toes, there shouldn't be any difficulty at all in meeting this target. All they have to do is to think independently and originally. Even so, there are many people in Japan who call themselves researchers, but who are incapable of following such thought processes. When we hire people we don't have to retrain them on technology. If we thought we would have to, we probably wouldn't hire them in the first place. But what we have to do is retrain them in the way they think. They have to be taught to follow the paths they want to and not just wait to be told what to do.

'It is strange, but maybe because the younger generation has had everything handed to them on plates, they are losing the ability to think independently. Ten years ago, we didn't have a problem in this area. The people who joined Canon did so because they wanted the freedom to work in areas they chose. Nowadays, unfortunately, we see a lot of people who are good when told what to do, but who are incapable of working alone.

'We don't hire people who need constant supervision and guidance, but, even so, nowadays we can only expect about two out of each hundred researchers to be capable of making creative leaps. This number has dropped considerably. Twenty years ago we could have expected twenty out of a hundred to be capable of such progress.

'I can only put this down to the failings of the Japanese education system which stifles individuality. Kids are simply not taught to be independent. Unless this changes, things are going to get even worse. I wouldn't be surprised if the number of truly original-thinking researchers drops as low as one in a thousand.

'In a way that is why we have to insist on a four-patents-a-year law. It ensures that our researchers don't just take advantage of their freedom to relax and do nothing. It prepares them for the total intellectual independence we promise. Until they have learned the responsibilities of freedom, they can't be given it.

'Ironically, another serious problem we are facing is the burgeoning of information availability. The Internet is a damned nuisance and a blocker of creativity. There is so much information on the Net today that many of the young researchers spend too much time finding out what other people have done, and just following along those lines. Despite what people say, the Internet damages originality rather than strengthening it. I try to discourage our young engineers from spending too much time on the Net. I tell them to read and think about their own original technologies.

'In the Meiji Period, a hundred years ago, Japan needed to catch up, and there was so much to do that the number of original and creative researchers was phenomenal. They had to be original because there just wasn't the amount of knowledge available to allow them merely to copy. People then were superb. Take, for example, the Meiji scholar Torahiko Terada, a professor at Tokyo Imperial University. He taught not only physics but also marine technology and meteorology. Now, that is what I call a truly rounded scholar. What I'm trying to do here is to get my staff to emulate Terada, in that they need to have a wide understanding of many subjects before they can concentrate on one. But the younger people today don't read books that can lead to original thought, they just stare at lists of data on computer screens.

'I tell them that they need to learn from the past, not just copy the latest crazes; that they need to read old books, not just look at the newest ideas or the latest technologies. In the older technologies are the seeds of the newest. For example, the basic technology for Liquid Crystal Displays (LCDs) was known in 1887. Edgar Allan Poe described it over a hundred years ago. There are literally thousands of research ideas out there in literature alone, but if the younger people continue only to look at sterile statistics, I don't hold out much hope for future technological breakthroughs.'

One of Canon's methods of combating researcher stagnation is to employ mid-career researchers from other companies and organizations. This not only brings a fresh approach to some areas of research, but also ensures a high level of enthusiasm. Many Canon researchers have come from elsewhere and recognize the much higher levels of freedom that they now have, with the result that they work extremely hard to repay the company for its faith in them.

One such researcher is Dr Nobuko Yamamoto, an associate scientist at R&D Headquarters. Her story is not untypical of Japan. After getting her Ph.D. in biotechnology, she worked for the National Cancer Research Institute, but didn't feel she was getting anywhere. She explains: 'Having a doctorate could actually be regarded as a disadvantage for a woman. I wasn't offered the jobs that I wanted, and was vastly over-qualified for the ones that were available to a woman. Particularly because I had a small child at the time, I felt as if I had only two choices. I could either go abroad and work where I would be appreciated, or run back home with my tail between my legs.

'It was while I was in this state that Dr Hajime Mitarai, then the head of research, contacted me and offered me a job, here at the Research Center, in my specialty area of biotechnology. Of course I jumped at the opportunity, even though I was staggered at actually being offered the job. I was even further surprised to hear that Dr Mitarai thought women often made better researchers than men.' This was probably the first time in her life that her sex had actually been an advantage for her. Even then it wasn't easy for her. 'Unlike nowadays,' continues Dr Yamamoto, 'when I joined there was no flex-time and the company didn't help in any way with child support. Even so, I was so happy to be here that I was determined to make the company thankful they had employed me. My choice of recent research was in gene identification. DNA is invisible, and to see and quantify it, we need to provide a light-emitting fluorescent dye which binds to the DNA. Ordinary dye, however, has bad resolution and a certain amount of background light is still shown, even if there is no DNA present. Together with my colleagues, we found a new dye for DNA staining that only allows light to be emitted when DNA is present. Canon hopes to use our discovery to eventually produce a DNA-based diagnostic system capable of spotting genetic or infectious diseases.

'The work that I have done at Canon may not only have a major effect on medicine, but, I hope, will pay the company back for having faith in me. I hope that what I have done has encouraged others to think more openly about employing women, but we have to face the fact that Japan is still a long way from sexual equality. Canon, however, is learning and leading.'

In R&D at least, as has been witnessed, Canon allows a high level of intellectual freedom. But as senior general manager Dr Takeshi Nakagiri says, he is worried about the quality of the new researchers Canon will be able to attract in the future. He doubts they will have the intellectual drive and originality to compete with their elders. Many in the company agree with him. Hajime Katayama, president of Amsterdam-based Canon Europa, believes that Canon is merely a microcosm of Japan in general. 'The Japanese have always been good at mass production, because there are strict orders that, if you follow them to the last detail, will make everything turn out correctly. But we have been very bad at the type of lateral thinking that is needed to make, for example, innovative software.

'This is partly because of our education system, which just teaches facts and statistics by rote, without educating anyone actually to think independently, but it is also down to the basic character of the Japanese, which is conservative and relatively unadventurous. That's why in the past much of our software research and development had to be done in the US or Europe. Japan in general, and Canon in particular, must encourage intellectual freedom and develop a system that will bring the free-thinkers to the top.'

Former Managing Director Tomomasa Matsui, now retired, believes there is still hope, for Canon at least, if not for Japan as a whole. 'If I was asked, I would say that Canon's strongest point is its offering of intellectual freedom. All members of staff at all levels are free to express their ideas, and can reasonably expect to be listened to. People are judged on their performance, not their family, school or birthplace. Unlike many Japanese companies, Canon's lack of cliques has given us the intellectual freedom to face the challenges of a constantly evolving world.'

This constantly and rapidly evolving world is what concerns *Nikkan Kogyo Shimbun* reporter Toru Arai. 'The development of the next new business areas for Canon will be critical. Until now, the company has managed to grow through the introduction of revolutionary and patented new technologies. But nowadays growth and new technology introduction will be slower and more incremental.

'In top management everyone seems to be optimistic about the possibility of future breakthroughs, and because of this, the regular employees also tend to look on the bright side of things. But with the world changing so quickly, Canon's speed of development may not be enough. Alliances with American and European companies may become necessary for survival. This is not necessarily a big problem, but Canon certainly needs to be careful.'

On the other hand, says Hiroshi Yoshihara, vice-president of Equity Research at Salomon Brothers Asia Limited in Tokyo, brilliant technological breakthroughs are not necessarily everything they are made out to be. 'Often Japanese companies are insultingly called copy-cats. But that is not necessarily bad for the balance sheet. In the product field it always seems that Matsushita is trying to catch up with Sony, but when it comes to the balance sheet, Matsushita is much, much bigger than Sony.' In Canon's case, it is often the company by which others are judged technologically. But in reality, we should look much more at the balance sheet and the product spread. In this respect, with the exception of software, Canon is almost unbeatable.

If he is correct, Canon's top management may be able to relax a little, but in a world where technological breakthroughs are the rule rather than the exception, they won't be able to afford to slow down too much. Canon is a company that has always been proud of its R&D abilities, and if it is subsiding into a more gentle middle age, the shareholders may well have cause for concern.

CHAPTER NINE

'Several years ago, an aeroplane ran out of fuel and crashed. After an inquiry it was discovered that the cause of the crash was a simple one-way valve in the fuel system. It had been put in the wrong way round, thereby fatally cutting off the fuel supply. The problem hadn't occurred before because the manufacturers had purposely threaded the valve in such a way that it could only be fitted correctly. However, in this case the service engineer had not trusted the translation of the service manual and had been convinced that the valve should go in the other way round. Obviously, when he tried to insert it he failed, because the threads were incorrect. But instead of accepting the foreign manual, he carefully rethreaded the valve, inserted it into the fuel system – and caused the plane to crash.'

This story is told by Dr Paul Otto, the British director of UK-based Canon Research Centre Europe Ltd. He doesn't, however, use it as an example of a language barrier problem. On the contrary, he says this is simply proof of the fact that wherever there is a human element, something is almost bound to go wrong. Dr Otto's beliefs are very similar to those held by Canon President Fujio Mitarai. He will not allow language barriers to be blamed for corporate failures, insisting that much more trouble is caused by a dearth of cultural knowledge than by the lack of a common tongue.

Born in the Mitarai home town of Oita, Kyushu, Fujio Mitarai comes from a family which produced many medical doctors, one of whom – Takeshi Mitarai, his uncle – was a founder of Canon, as seen in Chapter Two. Like many young people at that time, he moved away from his country home to Tokyo, where he enrolled in the law department of Chuo University. By the time he graduated, however, and at a time when Japan's economy was really beginning a sustained period of rapid and massive growth, the attraction of a career in business became more compelling. Now, from his position at the top of one of Japan's leading companies, he looks back with a certain amount of irony at the young man of those days in early 1961. 'I wasn't that ambitious at that time. What I dreamed of was, perhaps, getting promoted as high as the manager of our Kyushu branch. I never even considered going abroad. But within five years I was to start a residency in America that lasted for twenty-three fruitful years.'

Although he now looks back on those years with pleasure and pride, he wasn't always so positive about internationalization in general, and Americans in particular. In a November 1995 interview in the Japanese business magazine *Diamond*, Mitarai says, 'I spent twenty-three years in America and am extremely thankful that I have had the opportunity to understand and experience two very different cultures. But when I first went there, it was far from comfortable. America at that time was very rich and Japan was still relatively poor. Japanese expatriates were only allowed to take $200 a month out of the country, and I had to live on that. Even in those days, though, a cheap lunch of *tendon* (pieces of *tempura*, deep-fried fish and vegetables, on a bed of rice) would cost $3.00, so I never seemed to have any money to spare. I was always trying to borrow money and my only extravagance, after an eighteen-hour day, was to take a cab home from the office. And I only did that because I was scared of going on the subways.'

The cost of living wasn't the only thing that made this far from internationalized young businessman uncomfortable. Mitarai explains: 'When I first went to America I couldn't speak

English. In fact, I hated the language. At first, when Canon asked, I told them I didn't want to go, but my father ordered me to do what I was told, so I really had no choice. The obvious result of this was that because I didn't understand the language, I didn't allow myself to trust the Americans. This remained a problem until I learned to communicate with them. Then things changed.

'As I've said, when I first arrived in the US I wasn't very keen on Americans. But as I worked with them I began to notice things. For example, I had expected them to be hostile towards the Japanese because of the war. And, I suppose, I expected a certain arrogance because they'd beaten us. But this wasn't so. The Americans who were working for me were very cooperative and did what they were told without any complaints. It was then that I realized we were all working together and supporting each other for the common good.'

This realization of Mitarai's came many years before Ryuzaburo Kaku promulgated his *kyosei* theory (see Chapter Four), but as his language and communication skills improved, Fujio Mitarai understood the meaning of that philosophy – living and working together for the common good. And once he had accepted the fact that Americans, though different, were not enemies, he began to enjoy life. He explains: 'I made many American friends through work and golf. Though I disliked America when I arrived, I loved it by the time I left twenty-three years later. My time there was an experience that changed my life and my philosophy.

'America,' he continues, 'is a melting-pot of different races and religions. A nation of individualism: free and competitive. You either win or lose. But I also found out that individualism can equate to loneliness, so in some ways America can be a very severe place. Japan, on the other hand, is a typical Confucianist island nation. Responsibility is shared. And there is only one race and one language. It is comfortable, safe and cushioned. In a way,

America and Japan each has what the other lacks. America has raw energy and vitality, and Japan has a more philosophical view.

'The Japanese tend to look at America and judge it by Japanese standards, but you can't do that. I only really learned this after I'd been there for about ten years. That's why nowadays I tell my staff that if they go abroad, they should stay for at least ten years. You don't learn anything by staying two or three years. It is not just a matter of language, it is about culture.'

It is, perhaps, the ability to understand and live in both Western and Eastern cultures that will give Fujio Mitarai the management strengths he needs to lead Canon into the next century. He took over as president, unexpectedly, he claims, after the sudden death of his cousin, Hajime Mitarai. However, Hajime had only been president for just over two years (March 1993 to August 1995) and, at the time of his death, was only really beginning to make his mark on the company. So Fujio not only had to move surprisingly quickly up the ladder, he had to fill a vacuum with his own personality, philosophy and plans.

Even during the Hajime Mitarai presidency, the dominant figure at Canon had been Chairman Kaku. Toru Arai says, 'Kaku could best be described not as a businessman but as the soul and conscience of Canon. He was just as influential in Canon as the Pilgrim Fathers were in America.'

This philosophical metaphor can be carried even further and quite aptly applied to Ryuzaburo Kaku's love of China. Like the Chinese Mandarins of old, he was now above the fray of day-to-day business, and simply studied and philosophized about the future. Fujio Mitarai had very quickly to organize and expound his own theory of practical, here-and-now management. Few people knew what to expect. After all, he had been abroad for such a long time that some Japanese employees were worried that he would bring in a cut-throat form of American management.

But this was not to be. Arai explains: 'Before I met him and after I learned he had spent twenty-three years in the United States, I must admit I was expecting him to be rather Americanized. However, as soon as I saw him I realized that he was his own man, with his own philosophy, and that the years in America had not influenced him nearly as much as I had originally expected. He doesn't do business in an American way, nor in a Japanese way. He just does business in his own way – business with a human face.'

Some of the Western business watchers, however, seemed a little disappointed, not to say peeved. According to the *International Herald Tribune*, 'Despite his US experience, [new Canon President] Fujio Mitarai said he did not plan to adopt American business styles during his leadership, but [he also] said he would not be restricted to traditional Japanese business customs either.'

Mitarai's ability to distil a hybrid management style, combined with his modesty and humour, could be the key to his, and Canon's, future success. He explains his feelings on being made president. 'I was very shocked by the suddenness [of Hajime Mitarai's death]. He was so energetic, but his condition worsened very quickly. Being appointed his successor came as a surprise, but I felt that destiny was playing a part. I will do my best to be worthy of the responsibility I have been given.'

And his best included very quickly impressing his own character on Canon. He believes mainly in hard work, but understands that can only occur if the working environment is right. Toru Arai elaborates: 'Fujio Mitarai said, when he took over, "I'll make everyone work hard, no matter what age, young or old. But I can only do this if I provide them with a working environment in which they are stimulated to work hard. If I don't do this, then I should rightly be judged as a failure."'

Mitarai has no intention of failing, and soon made this clear when he laid out his plans for the future. He explains: 'We will carry on the process of globalization. We are now in the process of strengthening sales channels in China and other Asian countries, as well as production in Asia and Europe, including the UK. In addition, I will review our entire global manufacturing system with the aim of transforming the bulk of our production to the manufacturing of high-value-added products.

'As a further element of my globalization strategy, I will create a strong, well-balanced group of Canon companies. When I have achieved this, companies in economically strong regions can help compensate for the weaknesses of those suffering economic stagnation. It is vital that we all work together as a group.

'In the past, in the boom years, Canon's remarkable growth was as steady as a train running on rails. But looking at the harsh economic environment expected during the next few years, we will have to be more like the crew of a galleon at sea, all pulling together and using our combined skills and knowledge to ensure we move in the right direction.'

Within a few months of taking over, Mitarai had published his own five-year plan for Canon, with three major aims. First, he intends not only to foster the development of new businesses, but also to restructure existing departments, subsidiaries and affiliates that are not performing as well as hoped. This larger but leaner Canon, Mitarai believes, will be more fitted to face the rigours of the future. Second, he intends to introduce a new matrix management system that will bring together product groups and staff management functions. Through this he hopes to facilitate more effective and harmonious decision-making. Also, each of these new groups will be judged on how they contribute to Canon's overall consolidated profit. Finally, and this is where a little of his American experience is rubbing off, he intends to allocate responsibility for business units directly to company directors. Mitarai claims that making senior management directly responsible for the profitability of a product group will encourage them to show stronger and more innovative leadership than in the past.

Whether this will work or not, or just result in a lot of name-calling and scapegoating, remains to be seen. But Mitarai is very aware that, no matter how good a company's management is, or how idealistic its philosophy, if it doesn't have the products that the consumers want, it is in trouble. He is addressing the changing world of Japanese and global business.

'The world in general, and the world of business in particular,' he says, 'have undergone many changes over the years. Not so long ago, when you thought of industry you thought of heavy industries, such as steel and shipbuilding. But today the image of industry is different. Today's leading companies are in information technology. This is the new basic industry of our modern civilization and Canon's corporate strategy is to be in, and remain in, the vanguard of this industrial sector.

'The first building brick in Canon's future development is multimedia, or information technology. While we are not really involved in forming the infrastructure of the information society, we are deeply involved in many aspects, such as cameras (both conventional and digital) and printers, to mention just two. We are also developing and will soon commercialize a flat-display television screen. Next will be the world of semiconductors, and we are already in that business through our stepper machines. Finally there will be the businesses concerned with the safeguarding of the environment, particularly solar energy. This is an obvious business for the future, because fossil fuels are running out and cause massive pollution, and nuclear power is just not as safe as we once thought. Solar energy is the answer. It will not only benefit the developed nations but will also bring about faster development in Third World countries which find it almost impossible to meet the cost of fossil-fuel power. We are going to lead the field in the development of solar energy.

'The three keywords of the next century, therefore, will be: multimedia, semiconductors and environment. There is one particular area where we may expect to see some startling breakthroughs, and that is in the development of new software. Currently most of our software R&D is done in Japan, but we are annually investing more and more funds to pay for research in other countries, both through our own research centres and in cooperation with universities and other research facilities.

'However, while development and diversification are no doubt good things, we also have to keep a grip on our core technologies. Without these we just wouldn't exist. For example, Canon started out as a camera manufacturer, and even today two of our latest product groups, steppers and digital cameras, both use the years of knowledge we have accrued in optical technology.'

Canon management around the world seems to be almost in unison with Mitarai's plans, even though there are also some local aims and worries.

Canon Virginia President Michiaki Matsuo says, 'I would like to restructure our American manufacturing organization so that we can avoid a top-heavy bureaucratic system. I want to allow our employees to optimize their energy and vitality in ways best suited to them, and large bureaucratic organizations usually prevent that from happening. One of the better ways to accomplish this task is to establish additional subsidiaries.' Matsuo's comments reflect a continuing concern of Canon management, that the company is getting too bureaucratic and top heavy to react quickly to changing market conditions.

Ichiro Endo, the genius behind the BJP (Bubble Jet Printer), also worries about communication between researchers in the ever-growing giant corporation. 'In R&D we are already witnessing a borderless world. We already have five research centres overseas and must learn to fully utilize the best talents we can find, no matter where in the world. It is also important that we maintain a level of area pride. If, for example, a new technology is developed in the UK, it should be commercialized there and exported to other markets on demand. This way we keep the individualism and strengths of our various national companies at peak performance and maintain a high level of morale.' President Hajime Katayama of Canon Europa also stresses the importance of global localization. 'President Mitarai understands that Canon needs to become a truly global company with total understanding of individual markets. He also sees that if Canon is to succeed better than any other company around the world, the different areas or countries must be given their own heads and allowed to be run with local management and employees.'

Naoki Sato, director of Japanese Equity Research at Deutsche Morgan Grenfell, goes even further than Katayama. He thinks that the foreign market is vital to the survival of Canon, not only as a global trader but as a player on the Japanese market. 'Probably in Canon's view their subsidiaries and affiliates in the US and Europe are fundamentally more important to them than their subsidiaries in Japan, because they will be able to support Canon Inc. headquarters, no matter what the Japanese economic conditions are.'

Employees in Japan are very aware of the country's need to remain competitive, and in general support President Mitarai's plans. One employee of the Shimomaruko headquarters says, 'Historically Canon has been a leading mass producer of good-quality products. But the period of mass production in Japan is over. It is simply too expensive. Even abroad in, say, ten to twenty years, I expect to see Canon move away from mass production and into more value-added product areas. Our labour-intensive businesses will have to change. Eventually we will get back to our founder Dr Takeshi Mitarai's original concept of giving something back to society, through, say, the introduction of solar technology. We have to face the fact that mass production is sometimes just an excuse for making a lot of something that is relatively worthless.'

A fellow worker sees another potential problem. 'Our first priority must be to enhance our customer relations. Because we have a separate sales company, and communication isn't always good, there can often be differences between what the customers actually want, and what the engineers and designers think they need. In the future there needs to be more liaison between engineers, the sales company and the customers.'

This worry is a constant one for the chairman of a leading Tokyo-based dealer of Canon office equipment. He explains: 'There is a tendency in Canon to make something without asking our opinion. It may be of excellent quality, but if the market doesn't want it, it's no good. They shouldn't just come to us and expect us to sell whatever they make. It would be much better if they asked us first what we thought we could sell.

'Canon also tends to concentrate only on the technology, not the overall performance. A copier customer, for example, is not happy if he has a potentially very fast machine, but one in which the paper keeps jamming. He'd rather have a slightly slower but jam-free machine. This is not to say that Canon makes copiers that jam, of course, but occasionally a more down-to-earth attitude about machine performance would not go amiss. The engineers may be dreaming of the stars, but we have to sell on the earth.

'Also, Canon talk about globalization, but sometimes I think they are forgetting Japan. I really think they ought to look at getting out a few more products designed specifically for the Japanese market. After all, Japan still accounts for a third of their total sales. For example, I'd like to see a simple but fast copier, because right now Canon is good at the top end but hasn't got a product for the mass market. We'd also like to see a high-speed digital copier before everybody jumps on the bandwagon. I just hope somebody is listening to us. But even when all that has been said, I still think Canon have one of the best overall product ranges. If I didn't think so, I'd be looking at other products, and I'm not!'

Canon Europa's Katayama also has a little worry about local requirements. 'Hardware is pretty consistent the world over, so it can be made where it can be produced the cheapest. But software is a different matter. Software must be designed to give different value-added aspects in different societies, countries or applications. With software, we are not just shifting boxes, we should be supplying answers.' The chairman of the office equipment dealer supports this. 'Canon's weak point is mainly in the lack of very good software. They just don't seem to be very good at making quality interfaces with their hardware. They should take a few lessons from their competitors.'

Hiroshi Yoshihara, vice-president of Equity Research at Salomon Brothers Asia Limited in Tokyo, concurs. 'A possible problem for Canon is their inability to understand what the consumer wants. Of course engineers must believe that their products are the best and have the arrogance to say so. But sometimes the consumer is only interested in price and basic functions and isn't interested in getting the absolute latest technology. Because Canon is engineer-led there is a possibility of completely misjudging the market and launching products that simply aren't wanted – no matter how technologically excellent they are.'

Keisuke Fujita, general manager of one of Tokyo's largest camera retailing chains, Camera-no-Kimura, has the same worry. 'The problem with Canon is that because they are so big, if you have a complaint, they don't always seem to be able to find the time to listen. They tend to be stuck on their wonderful high technology and sometimes just don't realize the value of offering a complete package of workable equipment at a reasonable price.'

Yoshihara also worries about the attitudes of some employees.

He thinks they are typical of those working for large, successful organizations that have been growing fast, perhaps faster than is good for them. 'If Canon has another major problem, it is probably one of attitude more than anything else. They often seem to be very closed to outsiders, and can appear arrogant. I used to work for IBM some years ago, when it was unthought of that Big Blue could ever be in trouble. I remember the arrogance of IBM at that time and I sense a similar feeling in many Canon employees. I'm not saying that Canon will get into trouble, but that it would be better for them to know that even that is a possibility.'

To sum up Canon's prospects in the various product areas, Yoshihara says, 'Canon has to take care of its position. Xerox is aggressively catching up in the colour copier field, and may even be ahead in the area of digital technology. In printers Hewlett-Packard is number one and Canon looks like remaining second. In digital cameras Sony and other pure electronics companies are becoming more and more aggressive. Canon's strength really comes from what it can make in value-added sales such as printer cartridges. I don't think they are even close to finding a new technology area anywhere near as successful as their breakthrough in printer technology with the Bubble Jet. They will have to concentrate on improving what they have, rather than betting the farm on another major breakthrough.'

President Mitarai is well aware that technological leaps are probably not going to be as common in the future as in the past couple of decades. 'From now on,' he says, 'the process of development will be at a slower rate than in the past. Originally we made cameras, then added electronic devices for calculators and chemicals for printers. We had very few key technologies. But today we have very many technology areas and we expect to use them as incubators for good ideas, not as the tools from which we can expect quantum leaps in product development.'

Toru Arai thinks Canon may not even yet be taking the matter seriously enough. 'The development of the next new business area for Canon will be a problem. Until now the company has managed to grow through the introduction of revolutionary and patented brilliant new technologies. But nowadays growth and introduction will be slower and more incremental. In top management everyone seems to be optimistic about the possibility of future great breakthroughs, and because of this, the regular employees also tend to look on the bright side of things. But with the world changing so quickly, Canon's speed of development may not be enough. Alliances with American and European software and computer companies, in particular, may become very necessary for survival. This may not become a big problem, but it could do if the company is not careful.'

President Mitarai agrees that the future will not be easy, but is confident that Canon's policy of making *kyosei* strategic partnerships with both Japanese and non-Japanese companies will suffice to provide the talents not yet found within the company. He also feels that the more Canon's foreign subsidiaries and affiliates are left alone, the more they will grow to fill the gaps in Canon Inc.'s abilities. 'I think it would be ideal to have different faces of Canon in each country. In the main subsidiaries, manufacturing and sales should be vertically integrated and the top management should comprise local, non-Japanese people. Each subsidiary with its own culture should develop and manufacture their original products. These products could then be exported to other countries according to demand. Canon in the twenty-first century should be what I would describe as an internal network company.'

The internal but global network Mitarai is planning will become more and more focused on Asia in the coming years. He says, 'What excites me about the Asian market is its diversity. It combines highly developed markets like Hong Kong and

Singapore with many that are just emerging. But, big or small, each market shares a common thread: the presence of a growing middle class. This is a clear sign that we should accelerate our marketing efforts.'

The Asia 15 Project aims at considerably increasing sales throughout Asia each year from now until the end of the century. In 1996 Asia and Oceania represented about 8 per cent of Canon's $22 billion in sales. America, Europe and Japan divided up almost all the rest on a practically equal basis. The Asia 15 Project, Mitarai's own brainchild, has the target of reaching 15 per cent of sales in that area by the year 2000. He is very optimistic about the future of Asia. 'We are currently building up sales in the developing economies of Asia, particularly China. They are not rich now, but there is a good chance they will be in the next century. If peace prevails throughout Asia, which I think it will, consumption in the area is likely to expand at such a pace that it will relatively quickly surpass that of the States.

'Our aim in Asia, as in the rest of the world, is decentralization. We intend to have independent units operating in every country throughout the area. That is the aim, but it is not achievable in the very short term, because the people we need to employ will have to learn about and understand the Canon way of doing business. The Japanese at Canon will be involved, of course, because we are still a Japan-based company, but this is not necessarily a good thing, and we will be looking for managers of any nationality as long as they are multicultural.'

In the short term, however, while Canon is looking for and training these non-Japanese future managers, the company will have to rely on sending more and more people abroad from head office. Two years ago the Asia Training Programme was set up, again on Mitarai's orders. He explains: 'I really believe that Canon's approach to sending people abroad, particularly to Asia, makes us pioneers. We don't just send anyone.' The company set out its needs and demands in an internal recruitment brochure distributed in 1995. It described the aims and intentions as follows: 'As the Asian economy is expected to grow rapidly, Canon needs specialists who are fluent in native languages and customs. The training will be for two years. Before being sent to study overseas, the trainee will have two months' language training in Japan. Then, during the first year, the trainee will study the language at a school or university in the country of choice. The second year will be spent in-country at a Canon subsidiary. The qualifications are as follows: the applicant must be over twenty-five but under thirty, have worked for Canon for at least three years, have a strong desire to work in Asia, and be willing to go there alone, without family, for the two-year training period.'

The appeal worked, and some employees have already completed their training and are awaiting assignment to their new specialist countries. There was actually more enthusiasm than expected. Also, there was a refreshing diversity of reasons for wanting to be sent to Asia – more than normally exhibited by Japanese.

One applicant said, 'I've always been overwhelmed by the power of the Asian people. Japan seems so much weaker in terms of energy. I wish to spend as much time as I can with the Chinese in order to understand and, perhaps, emulate the power and strength of the people.' Another seemed more intent on communication. 'I will do my best to learn the language during my two years in Thailand. I want to express my opinions in the native language, and after studying the local culture and business customs, I hope to become an expert on Asian business.' A third, unusually for a Japanese, professed brotherhood. 'I applied for the Asia Training Programme because I am myself an Asian, and I like Asia. I have travelled to many countries already. During my two years as a trainee, I am sure I will get to know and like Asia more than before. I wish to work together with other Asians, and support them, and make them happy.' A fourth applicant, as well as being a realist in business terms, hadn't ruled out the possibility of a good time, saying, 'You cannot think of Canon's future without the Asian market. I wish to be fluent in Chinese so that I can argue with native Chinese, and also improve my mah-jongg skills.'

President Mitarai is also a realist about Japan's role in Asia, particularly in relation to China. 'I have seen American industry decline as Japan's grew. Japan will go through the same suffering with its relationship with South-East Asia and China. It can't be helped because it is fate. I stress to my employees the three Js, *ji-hatsu, ji-kaku* and *ji-chi* (self-motivation, self-awareness and self-management), and hope through these we can be good for ourselves, Canon and Asia.'

There is little doubt that Canon is choosing a sensible route to follow into the next century, but Toru Arai thinks the company may find it much more difficult than expected. 'Success in Asia will be different from that achieved in the US or in Europe. The Asians have close cultural as well as economic links with Japan, but even so it will need much more effort than in America or Europe to get the thing really moving. Canon will have to make a very significant effort, not just in money but in personnel and psychology.

'The company will have to study Asia very deeply if it wants to succeed. When everything is ready, Canon will really have to commit to localization. For example, there are still some countries in Asia that have very restrictive regulations concerning foreign currency. Many companies use their influence with national governments to get around such regulations. However, Canon doesn't like that way of going about things, so it may have some difficulties competing with other Japanese and foreign companies. If it was a level playing field and free competition, Canon would probably wipe the floor with their competitors. But trade in Asia isn't free, no matter what people say.'

Arai may be a little doubtful, but Mitarai is certain that the twenty-first century will belong to Asia, and intends to make sure that Canon is a major player. But how does he feel about the future of Japan itself?

'On the surface Japan seems to be beset by many problems, including political scandals, such as housing loan industry mis-management, a doubtful banking sector, and many others. But when you look at the economy in general, earnings are high, savings are as strong as ever, and there is little disparity in wage levels, so I can't help but feel that the real economy is not as bad as many doomsayers would have us believe.

'Also, Japan is still the world's greatest creditor nation, so short-term bad news doesn't necessarily worry the general public. And finally, we have a fantastic strength in the technological and scientific areas, so we are planning and building the products of the future. Really, if the government and private industry hold everything together, I think the future is looking pretty good.

'Canon is in an even better position than Japan as a whole. We are strong internationally and globally competitive, so we should be able to adapt to whatever circumstances arise. After all, if things turn bad in Japan, we can't move the country; but we can move Canon!'

The last word on the future, should perhaps go to Salomon Brothers' Yoshihara. 'Currently Canon is in the transition stage from a second division player to a top division company. It has not yet shed the image of a small, technology-led organization and taken on the clothes and actions of a giant, multinational concern. It seems a little unsure of its true position in the world.'

CHAPTER TEN

'Canon, like Honda and Sony, is controlled by men of charisma. However, unlike the other two companies, Canon has an identification problem. It may be one of Japan's most successful organizations, but when I tell people I'm writing a series on Canon, they still ask me, "What does Canon actually do? What really is Canon?"' So says Toru Arai, the *Nikkan Kogyo Shimbun* journalist who has probably studied Canon more deeply than any other Japanese writer.

And after almost 200 hours of interviews with Canon staff throughout Japan, Asia, Europe and America, backed up by visits to company facilities throughout the world, I still wonder if I have an answer to the question of what Canon really is. Certain facts are obvious. Canon has 75,628 employees worldwide, with just over half based in Japan. Its annual sales, in the last year for which figures were available at the time of writing, totalled over $22 billion, which comprise $1.8 billion in Asia and Oceania and the rest almost equally divided between Japan, Europe and the United States. In 1996 Canon (1,541) was second only to IBM (1,867) in the number of US patents granted, and has never dropped below fifth place in any year of the decade. And Canon has marketing and/or manufacturing subsidiaries or affiliates throughout Asia, Oceania, Europe and the Americas. Of this much we can be certain. But what really is Canon?

In some ways, Canon can be seen as a typical Japanese growth company. Having started in the thirties, it stagnated during the war, only to rise from Tokyo's ashes with renewed vigour. With the help of the Occupation Forces, Canon re-established itself as a leading Japanese camera maker, and began flexing its manufacturing muscles towards the end of the 1940s.

The 1950s started with a short period of consolidation, followed by years of innovation and expansion. American and European sales offices were opened, and global distribution contracts were signed. New products came off the production lines one after the other, and each seemed to be packed with yet more technological innovation than the last. Towards the end of the fifties, Canon took several steps into the unknown, through investment in totally new technologies and manufacturing processes. From cameras and lenses, the company attempted to diversify into electronics, with the introduction of the Synchroreader recording device, and electronic calculators.

Although the foray into the world of recording devices was soon abandoned, Canon refused to retreat to its core technologies, and persevered with calculator introductions. Eventually, though, the 1970s brought failure in this market as well. The lessons learned in developing these two new technologies were then noted when a new area of diversification was planned. And this time it was even more successful than the company could have hoped.

By the early 1970s, Canon was well established as a major player in the electrophotographic copier machine market, a position it has continued to strengthen to this day. Furthermore, Canon's researchers have continued to explore and commercialize many other product fields, much to the benefit of the company's balance sheet. It cannot be doubted that Canon is one of Japan's, perhaps the world's, greatest technological innovators.

But therein also lies a past, and potential future, problem. Canon has been, and to a certain extent still is, engineer-led. Reporters, distributors, analysts and retailers can't all be wrong when they complain of Canon's occasional arrogance. There is clearly a lesson here for the company to take to heart, in that it should attempt to take a little more notice of what its customers actually want. Instead of making products that Canon think consumers should buy, it is time that the company considered improving its market research capabilities. 'It is occasionally like trying to sell the customer a Rolls-Royce when he only wants a Robin Reliant,' says one British retailer. 'It is no good me telling him how superior the technology in the Rolls-Royce is, if he is only interested in, or can only afford, the basics of the Reliant.'

On the other hand, Canon has got where it is today only by insisting on the very highest specifications on all its products and never accepting second-best. So the company's arrogance may perhaps be justified after all. And in fact top management seems to comprise a great number of pragmatists and realists. Not for them the path of arrogance and ivory towers. They see the world as it is, predict what it is going to become, and lay their plans accordingly.

In this respect, Canon has been extremely fortunate in its directors. From its very early days the company has been led by men of vision. Takeshi Mitarai, one of the founders and perhaps, along with Ryuzaburo Kaku, the most influential person Canon ever had, started the Canon style and inaugurated a kind of philosophy extremely rare in corporate culture.

Mitarai's medical background gave him an outlook on life and business that was very different from that of the average tycoon. He believed in working for the good of society and instilled this creed in almost everyone he came across. The CEOs that followed him, including his American-educated son, Hajime Mitarai, and his nephew, current president Fujio Mitarai, continued this humanistic approach to business.

In some ways humanism, that is, caring for humanity, can be translated as paternalism, and that is very common in Japanese corporations. Here, though, Canon yet again differs from many other Japanese companies. Although in the eyes of some of the foreign employees, and a few of the Japanese, Canon is a little too paternalistic and interfering, it is markedly less so than the majority of Japanese organizations.

. In this company, less so than in many others, although Daddy keeps an eye on things, he isn't always around to interfere in every aspect of the business. Once his employees have learnt their jobs and the Canon way, he leaves them very much alone to get on with it. In fact, Takeshi Mitarai and other presidents have insisted on Canon employees being as independent as possible. They are taught to observe the company's Three-Js philosophy of *ji-hatsu, ji-kaku* and *ji-chi* (self-motivation, self-awareness and self-management). But this doesn't mean that Canon employees are simply left to fend for themselves. They aren't. They are seen to belong to the greater Canon family. And this doesn't just refer to Japanese employees. Those working for Canon throughout the world are given a lot more freedom to do what they think is best than in almost any other Japanese company I have known. They are shown that their company believes in them, and that they shouldn't expect to be watched over at all times. This seems to work well, says Martin Laws, managing director of Canon UK. 'Canon leave me very much alone to make my own decisions, but if I need advice, they are always ready and willing to help.'

This respect for the individual is typical of Canon, not only in Japan and the industrialized West, but anywhere that the company operates. The company tries to allow all its employees to maintain dignity. For example, the management of Canon Inc. in Tokyo hope that all non-Japanese subsidiaries will eventually be managed by locals, and that all Tokyo will then have to do is be prepared to help and advise. This may be a long way off yet, but at least Canon has embarked on the journey. Already several

American and European companies have local heads, and many others have potential CEOs understudying the role. Many Japanese companies have an apparent in-built abhorrence of putting non-Japanese in charge, but Canon doesn't seem to suffer from this.

Under Chairman Kaku, Canon adopted the *kyosei* philosophy of living and working together for the common good. I have to admit that when I first heard about it I was more than a little sceptical. So many times over the years I have heard the leaders of Japanese multinational corporations publicly embracing the philosophy of brotherly love and internationalization just before they close a foreign outlet.

All too often, Japanese business leaders don't really care what happens to their foreign workers. After all, they are far away from Japan, so they can't become thorns in the corporate side. Canon, though, seems to mean what it says, not only about looking after its employees, wherever they are, but also about preserving the environment in which they work and live. Having said this, however, last year's strike by Canon workers in France shows that the company hasn't necessarily got it right yet, no matter how much it appears to be trying.

It is unlikely that any company, anywhere in the world, takes quite as much care to safeguard the natural environment. Only the highest standards are allowed at any Canon factory, and there is no difference in standards between Canon factories in China and California. This in itself is unusual for a Japanese company. In most cases, only the environmental standards of the country where the plant is actually sited are obeyed, and a Third World installation would never be as clean or as safe as an equivalent Western plant.

This respect and care for the environment may also be traceable to the personal life of Chairman Kaku. A survivor of the Nagasaki atom bombing, he cares very deeply about pollution and the suffering it inevitably brings. And this is also one of the main reasons why Canon is investing so heavily in solar energy research. Most directors don't expect to see a profit from this side of the business for many years, possibly not even during their working lives. But the research goes on, and, according to the company, will not stop until all the problems have been solved and the technology commercialized.

So we have a company that cares for its people and their families, looks after the environment, and tries to foster independent thought and respect for society. Is Canon, then, the perfect corporate citizen of the twenty-first century? I doubt it. In fact, I doubt if such perfection will ever be reached by any company.

Canon is, after all, a company looking for profits. It is not a charity, and if push comes to shove, and times get really hard, I doubt that a philosophy of equality and humanity will survive. But I may be wrong, and, after all my meetings with Canon people throughout the world, I'm more than a little hopeful that I am being over-pessimistic. There is definitely still a strong possibility that Canon, a transliteration of Kannon, the Buddhist Goddess of Mercy, may not be an inappropriate name after all.

CHRONOLOGY

1933	Canon's predecessor, Precision Optical Instruments Laboratory, founded
1934	Kwanon 35mm camera developed
1935	Registration of 'Canon' trademark
1937	Precision Optical Industry Co. Ltd founded
1939	In-house production of Serenar Lens commences
1940	Japan's first Indirect X-ray camera developed
1947	Company becomes Canon Camera Co. Inc.
1951	Head office and manufacturing plants concentrated in Shimomaruko, Ohta-ku, Tokyo
1955	New York branch office opened
1957	Canon Europa established
1961	'Electric-eye' boom sparked by introduction of Canonet
1962	Develops first five-year plan
1964	Canola 130, the world's first 10-key electronic calculator, introduced
1966	Canon USA Inc. established
1967	Canon Latin America established
	Ratio of exports to net sales surpasses 50 per cent
1968	Canon Amsterdam NV (today, Canon Europa) established
1969	Company's name changed to Canon Inc.
	Canon Research Center established in Japan
1970	Canon Inc., Taiwan, established
	NP-1100, Japan's first plain paper copying machine, introduced

1971	Canon Sales Co. Inc. formed
1972	Canon Giessen GmbH established
1973	Japan's first full-colour plain paper copying machine introduced
1975	Develops laser beam printer (LBP)
1976	First Premier Company Plan launched
	AE-1 camera with a built-in microprocessor introduced
	CR-45NM non-mydriatic retinal camera introduced
1979	Overseas sales exceed ¥100 billion ($450 million)
	LBP-10, using a semiconductor laser, introduced
	AF35M, 'Sure Shot', fully automatic AF compact camera, introduced
1981	World's first Bubble Jet printing technology announced
1982	Second Premier Company Plan launched
	PC-10 and PC-20, world's first personal copying machines with replaceable cartridges, introduced
1984	Digital Laser Copying machine system NP-9030 introduced
	LBP-8/CX, world's smallest and lightest LBP, introduced
1985	BJ-80 Bubble Jet printer introduced
1987	Canon Foundation established
	CLC-1 digital full-colour copying machine introduced
	EOS autofocus SLR system introduced
1988	Global Corporation Plan, introducing *kyosei* philosophy, launched
	Canon Research Centre Europe Ltd established in UK

1990	Committee to promote environmental assessment established
	Cartridge recycling programme launched
	BJ-10 series of Bubble Jet notebook-size printers introduced
1991	World's first display based on the ferroelectric liquid crystal (FLC) technology developed
1992	CLC-550, equipped with the world's first anticounterfeit technology, introduced
	GP55 digital copying machine introduced
	BJC-820 full-colour Bubble Jet printer introduced
	EOS5, world's first eye-controlled autofocus camera, introduced
1993	Ecology Research and Development Center begins operations
1994	35mm cameras pass the 80 million production mark
1995	'Asia 10' project launched
	CS (customer satisfaction) Promotion Committee formed
	Earns certification under the BS7750 international environmental standard
1996	Excellent Global Corporation Five-Year Plan initiated
	Operations begin at Fuji-Susono Research Park in Japan

INDEX

GLOBAL RESPONSIBILITIES AND LOCAL DECISIONS

Otto, Dr Paul 142

packaging 78
Palo Alto, California 74
Panther series of electronic calculators
    90–91
paternalism 97–8, 161–2
Pearl Harbor attack (1941) 24, 52
Pearl spring camera 20, 23
Percy, Charles H. 107–8
Pickens, T. Boone 117
plain paper copier (PPC)
    manufacture 12, 88, 130
plastics 78
Platt, Lewis H. 68
Poe, Edgar Allan 138
Poland 74, 126
pollution 60, 64–5, 77, 148, 163–4
Polly Peck 117
post-electrophotography 130–31
PPC *see* plain paper copier
    manufacture 88
precision engineering 89
precision optical engineering 90
Precision Optical Industry Co., Ltd *see*
    Seiki Kogaku Kogyo Co., Ltd
Precision Optical Instruments
    Laboratory *see* Seiki Kogaku
    Kenkyusho
precision optics 89
Premier Company Plan (*yuryo kigyo*)
    adoption of 91
    initial aims 13
    Kaku describes the success of 11
    Kaku presents his concept 9–10
    mistranslated as 'Blue-chip
      Company Plan' 13
    permeates Canon operations 14
    philosophy 13
    stages in achievement of 13, 15, 16
Prince Hotel, Shinagawa (Canon

directors' meeting, 1975) 7–11
printer cartridges 153
printers 148
    Bubble Jet 27, 59, 130–35
    ink jet 12, 69, 131
    laser-beam 67–9, 131
Product Development Headquarters
    130

Queensland, Australia 66

R&D Headquarters Canon Research
    Centre, Atsugi City 129–30,
    134, 138
rain-forests, depletion of the 78
recording technology 90, 130
recycling 78, 79
Ricoh 12, 13
Rockefeller Center 66
Rohra, Dr Aruna 99–100
Roppongi entertainment district,
    Tokyo 19
Russia 57

Sakimoto, Ms Yukiko 96
salcomycin 84
Salomon Brothers Asia Limited 86,
    141, 152, 158
Sato, Naoki 150
scanners 27
Schaumberg, Illinois 74
Scotland 74, 78–9
Second World War 23, 24, 159
Seiki Kogaku Kenkyusho (SKK;
    Precision Optical Instruments
    Laboratory)
    Asahi Camera advertisement 19–20
    first logo 21
    founded by Uchida and Yoshida 19
    Hansa Canon camera 22–3
    hires excellent engineers and
      designers 20

177

Seiki Kogaku Kenkyusho – *cont.*
  Kwanon range of cameras and
    lenses 20, 21, 22
  Mitarai bankrolls 36
  Mitarai recruited 20, 21
  Uchida's realism v Yoshida's
    idealism 21–2
Seiki Kogaku Kogyo Co., Ltd
    (Precision Optical Industry Co.,
    Ltd)
  absenteeism v loyalty during
    wartime conditions 28–9
  founded (1937) 23–4
  indirect X-ray camera production
    26, 38
  Mitarai's philosophy 25
  Takeshi Mitarai winds up the
    company (1945) 29
  Uchida severs his ties with 25
Seiko Epson 12, 13
semiconductors 126, 148, 149
sha-in 40, 42
Sharp 12, 88
SHEEP (code-name for small
    systems for laser-beam printers)
    131
Sheet Reader 85
Shimomaruko headquarters, Ohta-ku,
    Tokyo (for Japan and Asia) 5, 15,
    81, 83, 95, 97, 101, 106–7, 150
Shinjuku, Tokyo 6, 46–7
Shinkansen (Bullet Train) 81
Shintoism 128
Shoei 27
Shuinsen system 61
Singapore 24, 155
single-lens reflex (SLR) cameras 12,
    13, 23, 83, 110
Sino-Japanese War 46, 47, 49
SKK *see* Seiki Kogaku Kenkyusho
slide-rule 88
software 140, 141, 149, 152, 154

solar cell technology 59–60
solar energy 148, 150, 164
Sony 2, 34, 67, 141, 153, 159
South America 75
South-East Asia 157
Spain 74
stepper machines 12, 148, 149
Stomm, Dr Roderich Graf von 121,
    125
Suminokura, So-an 60–61
Supreme Command Allied Powers
    (SCAP) 30
Suzukawa, Hiroshi 111
Suzuki, Ms Asako 96
Suzuki, Teruo 129, 139
Sweden 74
Switzerland
  Canon marketing subsidiaries/
    affiliates 74
  chosen as Canon's European
    headquarters 82
  distribution 113
Synchroreader recording device 10,
    83–5, 87, 89, 160

Tadenuma, Masamitsu 47
Taiwan 99
Takemoto, Hideharu 69, 134
Takikawa, Seiichi 36, 38, 111
Tanaka, Hiroshi 89
Tanaka, Masahiro 105, 125
Tappahannock, Virginia 74
TEC 12
tera-bit memory 135
Terada, Torahiko 137
Texas Instruments 34
Todai-Kyodai (Tokyo University-
    Kyoto University) clique 51
Tokugawa Period 71
Tokyo
  after the Second World War 29
  Olympic Games (1964) 81, 87